Spanish for Beginners

Learn Spanish in 30 Days Without Wasting Time

Table of Contents

Introduction

¡Hola!

It's great to have you here! We're about to embark on a 30-day Spanish-learning journey that will take us from zero to fluent, and we're thrilled to have you on board!

If your Spanish classes aren't going at your desired pace or you feel that you're not learning what you need for your trip, this book was definitely made for you. We're here to help you *really* learn Spanish in a practical way.

Spanish is an incredible language with over 560 million speakers worldwide; it is constantly enriched by the different countries and cultures in which it is spoken. You won't want to miss the opportunity of learning how to chat with its speakers.

This book will take you from the basics to different situations where you might need to speak Spanish while visiting a Spanish-speaking country. Considering that Spanish is the official language of 21 countries, after completing this course, you should be able to converse easily while visiting many Spanish-speaking destinations.

Divided into 10 chapters, this book includes some grammar-made-easy guides for you to finally understand how to use the tenses, a pronunciation guide to learn how to sound like a native, and some exercises to practice as you go along. The grammar explanations are simple and easy to understand, the pronunciation guide contains hands-on instructions to attempt a better pronunciation, and the exercises will place you in real and likely scenarios for you to practice before your actual journey.

Since the book is practically divided, it will be really easy for you to find the perfect phrase for every moment of your trip. We will go over everything you need to know to be confident enough to tackle any scenario in Spanish. And you will find some fixed expressions for you to use, but you will also learn to use your own words to say what you mean.

Unlike other books that are only devoted to grammar and vocabulary, this book will also take you on a cultural journey since we're going to travel around and talk about Spanish culture, as well as learn some phrases to use in colloquial conversations.

So, what are you waiting for? Our 30-day journey awaits, and we want you to come out the other side speaking Spanish like a pro to everyone you meet.

¡Buen viaje!

Chapter 1: Spanish Basics

We told you we would build your Spanish from the ground up, so here we are! In this chapter, we will see *all* the basics so you can have a solid foundation for every situation you find yourself in. Even though this chapter will be about the basics, it might be the most important one, so pay attention!

I think it's also time to introduce ourselves. My name is Sarah. This year, for the summer holidays, I will be going on a 30-day trip to Spain with my friend Julio – who is not only Spanish but also a Spanish language teacher. Right now, all I know how to say is *hola* and *gracias*! So Julio will be teaching me everything I need to know to communicate on our trip!

Right now, we're at the airport. We bought a ticket for a plane that will take us from Hartsfield-Jackson airport in Atlanta, US, to El Prat Airport in Barcelona, Spain. We'll use the time in the airport and on the flight to get through some Spanish basics. So, I'll let Julio take over!

Brief History of the Spanish Language

Hi! I'm Julio, your Spanish friend and teacher for the next month. How about we start with the history of the language?

Spanish is a Romance language, meaning it derives from Latin (unlike English which is a West Germanic language). First, about 5,000 years ago, some people in Spain and the Iberian Peninsula started speaking various dialects. Then, the Romans introduced

Latin to what was then called Hispania. The combination of Latin with the previous dialects resulted in what is called *Vulgar Latin.*

In the Middle Ages, Spain was conquered by the Visigoths, who continued using Vulgar Latin. But then, the Muslim Empire conquered what is – today – the province of Andalusia. As this happened, Latin started taking shape into the Romance languages we know now (French, Italian, Romanian, Portuguese, and Castilian). The Arab occupation introduced some Mozarabic words into the language, and it was spoken in some regions.

Castilian was a language with Vulgar Latin and Mozarabic influences that later became the basis for the written standard, and it also became the language for administrative tasks, the establishment of decrees, and the writing of chronicles and legal works.

The Christian Catholic Kingdoms of Castilla, Aragon, Toledo, Galicia, Zaragoza, and Leon united to expel the Arabs. With this, the Mozarabic language eventually disappeared from the region. Isabella of Castile and Ferdinand of Aragon became the King and Queen of this unified Spain and were known as the Catholic Monarchs. After this, Castilian eventually became the official language in Spain.

Nowadays, Spanish is a very diverse language and isn't spoken merely in Spain. Actually, it is spoken in 21 countries around the world, and so, of course, the vocabulary, the pronunciation, and even some aspects of Grammar change from one country to another. But do you know why it is spoken in so many countries?

In 1492, the Catholic Monarchs gave Christopher Columbus the means to seek other routes to India. In the process, as we all know, he arrived on the American continent. With the arrival of the Spanish conquerors, the American civilizations were colonized and forced to take on the Spanish language, religion, and traditions.

Between 1492 and 1989, the Spanish Empire expanded across the Caribbean Islands, half of South America, most of Central America, and part of North America. Later, these countries would fight for independence, but most kept the Spanish language.

Today, there are over 560 million Spanish speakers worldwide – many found in non-Spanish-speaking countries like the United States.

Alphabet and Accents

Well, now that we know a bit of the eventful history of the Spanish language, let's learn about the language itself.

The alphabet in Spanish is almost the same as in English, except, of course, each letter has a different name, and there is also that thing about the mystical letter Ñ. Let's have a look at it!

A	B	C	D	E	F	G
a	*be*	*ce*	*de*	*e*	*efe*	*ge*
H	I	J	K	L	M	N
hache	*i*	*jota*	*ca*	*ele*	*eme*	*ene*
Ñ	O	P	Q	R	S	T
eñe	*o*	*pe*	*cu*	*erre*	*ese*	*te*
U	V	W	X	Y	Z	
u	*uve /* *ve*	*uve doble / doble u / doble ve*	*equis*	*i griega*	*zeta*	

As Sarah noticed, the V and the W have alternative names. Well, that's because depending on the Spanish speaker you are talking to, they might say it in one of these ways. Generally, in Spain, people usually say *uve* and *uve doble;* in Central America, *ve* and *doble u* are more common. In South America, *ve* and *doble ve* are the most common alternatives.

Now let's learn a bit about accents.

In Spanish, there is only one type of written accent called *tilde* which can only go on vowels and signals where the stressed syllable is (it is represented in this way: *á, é, í, ó,* and *ú*). However, not all Spanish words have *tildes,* because the rule isn't to simply graphically express every stressed syllable. Here is a table of the rules of accentuation in Spanish:

	Rule	Examples
Agudas	The stressed syllable of *agudas* is the last one. But they only need a *tilde* when the word ends in N, S, or a vowel.	*Agudas* with *tilde*: *canción, sofá, bebé, café, menú* *Agudas* without *tilde*: amar, mujer, salud, comer, sabor
Graves	The stressed syllable of *graves* is the second to last one. But, unlike *agudas*, they need a tilde when the word *doesn't* end in N, S, or a vowel.	*Graves* with *tilde:* azúcar, móvil, ángel, lápiz, ángel *Graves* without *tilde:* sonido, abrazo, cocina, saludo
Esdrújulas	The stressed syllable of *esdrújulas* is the third one starting from the end of the word. These are easy because they always need a *tilde*.	esdrújula, último, íntimo, política, sinónimo, sólido

I know, this seems like a lot to take in! But for the time being, you should remember that the stressed syllable is the one with the *tilde* - and if you have any doubts about which is the stressed syllable of a word, you can always return to this table.

Pronunciation Tips

Before we go any further into pronunciation - and before I give you some tips - I encourage you to go to the extra chapter called "IPA Phonemic Chart" to get acquainted with every Spanish sound individually and their phonemes.

Now, about those tips... The first one, as I will probably keep on repeating throughout this book, is that practice makes perfect! So don't feel discouraged if you don't get everything right at first, it might take some time, but you'll get the hang of it in no time.

Spanish is very different from English – but also much more straightforward. Even though some pronunciations may vary from place to place, in Spanish, the vowels are always pronounced the same way (and almost all consonants, except for a few exceptions).

So, once you've mastered the basic sounds and learned to roll your Rs, you don't need to wonder if you are saying the word correctly because you probably are!

Let's see a few comparisons between Spanish and English, so you get what I mean:

In English, the Es in "essence" are different from one another and from the E in "be," and also different from the Es in "Peter." But in Spanish, *esencia, ser,* and *pedro* all use the same pronunciation for the E.

Another example is the use of As in "apple," "saber," "seat," "saw," and "wait." They all sound different! Whereas in Spanish, the As in *manzana, sable, asiento, miraba,* and *esperar* all sound the same.

The vowels are not as straightforward when you find a U and an E together after a Q or a G. In these cases, you should pronounce them as an E, which means that the U is silent. And the same happens if you find a QUI or a GUI, you should pronounce the vowels as an I. Some examples of this are *queso, panqueque, quiero, saquito, guitarra, águila, guepardo* and *albergue.*

However, there is one little exception to this rule, but it is simple, *I promise!* Whenever there is a GÜI or a GÜE with those two little dots above the U (which, by the way, are called diaereses), it means that the U should be pronounced. Though this is not that common, some examples are *pingüino* and *vergüenza.*

Now, with the consonants, you should know that there are some exceptions, but it is still quite simple. Here they are:

- If we find an R at the beginning of a word or a double R in the middle, they both sound the same and are called rolled Rs! For example, we use rolled Rs in *ratón, correr, reliquia,* and *marrón.* But, if you find a single R in the middle or at the end of a word, that's not a rolled R. This R can be found in words like *amargo, cantar, broma,* and *prado.*

- Something similar happens with the L - it has one pronunciation when it is on its own and one when it's doubled. On its own, it sounds like an English L, like in *lago, salir, mal,* and *lejos.* But when it's doubled, it may have different pronunciations depending on the region (you can find information about this in the "IPA Phonemic Chart" chapter!), and it is used in words such as *lluvia, valla, llorar,* and *allí.*

- And lastly, there's the case of the G, which sounds different depending on what vowel comes after. It is a soft G when it is followed by an A, O, or U (including when a UI or a UE follows it), like in *gato, guisante, agua,* and *amigo.* But suppose an E or an I follow it. In that case, the pronunciation is more similar to a J, like in *gelatina, gitano, ángel,* and *agitar.*

- Something similar happens to the letter C. If it is followed by A, O, or U, it is pronounced as an English K. However, if an E or an I follow it, it is pronounced more like an English S.

Regarding consonants, the last tip I can give you is to remember that the H in Spanish is silent, *so don't try to pronounce it!*

Word order

Now we're getting closer to grammar; here's a summary of what happens with word order.

In affirmative sentences, word order in Spanish is very similar to word order in English - we usually have the subject first and then the verb with its complements, if it has any. Examples of this are: *Alejandro corre* ("Alejandro runs"), or *Sandra tiene mucho dinero* ("Sandra has a lot of money").

As a subject, we can have a person's name, but we can also have a pronoun, a word that refers to the person we are talking about (like *I, you,* or *she* in English). This is used only when we've been talking about this person, so the people in the conversation know who we are referring to.

Pronouns in Spanish are:

- First-person singular: *yo* ("I")
- Second-person singular: *tú* ("you")
- Third-person singular: *él / ella* ("he" / "she")
- First-person plural: *nosotros / nosotras* ("we")
- Second-person plural: *vosotros / vosotras / ustedes* ("you")
- *Third-person plural: ellos / ellas* ("they")

Using pronouns, the two previous examples can turn into *Él corre* ("He runs"), and *Ella tiene mucho dinero* ("She has a lot of money").

The thing about Spanish, though, is that the subject (whether a name or a pronoun) can be left out of the sentence if it is clear who we are talking about. So, if we were already talking about Sandra and then we say that she has a lot of money, we can simply say *Tiene mucho dinero* ("(She) Has a lot of money") without the need for an overt subject.

Another example of this using the first sentences could be in a conversation like this one:

– *¿Alejandro come en su tiempo libre?* ("Does Alejandro eat in his free time?")

– *No, corre.* ("No, (he) runs.")

Now, this example takes us to the word order of questions. In English, the order changes to signal a question, but in Spanish, for yes/no questions, we use the same word order, and we add an opening question mark to signal that a question has just started. For example, if we want to turn the statement *Juan quiere comer algo dulce* ("Juan wants to eat something sweet") into a question, we would simply add question marks: *¿Juan quiere comer algo dulce?* ("Does Juan want to eat something sweet?").

In the previous example, the direct object of the verb *comer* is *algo dulce*. Here, *algo* is a noun, and it is being modified by the adjective *dulce*, which describes *algo*. In Spanish, unlike in English, adjectives usually go after the noun and not before it. An example of this could be *Juan come una galleta dulce y deliciosa*, which in English would be "Juan eats a sweet and delicious cookie."

And in a sentence, there can also be adverbs, which are words that describe how the action is being made or say something about the verb. Just like adjectives come after nouns, in Spanish, adverbs usually come after verbs and even at the end of the whole sentence. So, we could say *Alejandro corre rápidamente* ("Alejandro runs fast") or *Juan come una galleta dulce y deliciosa lentamente* ("Juan slowly eats a sweet and delicious cookie").

In English, to join two clauses together in one sentence, we usually use conjunctions– words that connect the clauses. The most common ones in English are "and" and "but," whose Spanish counterparts are "y" and "pero" respectively. For example, we could join the two previous examples into one sentence in the following way: *Alejandro corre rápidamente y Juan come una galleta dulce y deliciosa lentamente* ("Alejandro runs fast and Juan slowly eats a sweet and delicious cookie").

Capitalization and Punctuation

Luckily, capitalization and punctuation in Spanish are very similar to those in English.

For starters, in Spanish, they use capital letters only at the beginning of a sentence, and with proper nouns, that is, with names. So, we will capitalize Alejandro, Sandra, and Juan, as well as other names like Barcelona, Madrid, and the Sagrada Familia. However, we do not capitalize common nouns, such as *iglesia, casa,* and *río.*

As for punctuation, it works the same way as in English, but there are a few differences. As we've seen, one of the differences is that question marks are doubled; that is, there should be one at the beginning and one at the end of a question. And the same happens to exclamation marks; they should always be doubled. For example, we can turn the statement *Ana tiene un perro* ("Ana has a dog") into a question by adding the question marks *¿Ana tiene un perro?* ("Does Ana have a dog?") or into an exclamation by adding the exclamation marks *¡Ana tiene un perro!* ("Ana has a dog!").

Another difference is that, in Spanish, the em dash (–) is not as common as in English, and it is only used as parentheses and never as a colon. This means that it should always be double and that the em dashes go right next to the words they are enclosing, like parentheses. For example: *Pipo–el perro de Ana–es muy lindo*

("Pipo – Ana's dog – is very cute").

Colors

Now it's time to learn a bit of vocabulary. These are all the colors you should know

- *Rojo* means "red"
- *Naranja* means "orange"
- *Amarillo* means "yellow"
- *Verde* means "green"
- *Azul* means "blue"
- *Púrpura* and *violeta* mean "purple" (which one is used depends on the region)
- *Rosa* means "pink"
- *Gris* means "gray"
- *Negro* means "black"
- *Blanco* means "white"
- *Magenta* means "magenta"
- *Celeste* means "light blue"
- *Turquesa* means "turquoise"
- *Marrón* means "brown"

Numbers 1-10

Now let's finish this chapter with numbers 1 to 10 in Spanish!

1. *uno*
2. *dos*
3. *tres*
4. *cuatro*
5. *cinco*
6. *seis*
7. *siete*
8. *ocho*
9. *nueve*
10. *diez*

Exercises

Now it's time to review everything we've seen so far to ensure you understand everything.

1. Sarah's full name is Sarah Williams, which in Spanish is spelled "ese-a-erre-a-hache uve doble-i-ele-ele-i-a-eme-ese."

   Can you spell out loud the word *mujer*? Why doesn't it have a *tilde*?

2. What does it mean if a vowel has a *tilde*?

3. What do the words *calor, país, alimentación,* and *salmón* have in common?

   a. They are all agudas

   b. They are all graves

   c. They are all esdrújulas

4. What does it mean if a word is a *grave*?

5. Regarding accents, what do the words *lápiz, soñar, cálido,* and *mano* have in common?

   a. They are all *agudas*

   b. They all have a *tilde*

   c. The stressed vowel is the A

6. If there is an R at the beginning of a word (like in *receta*), should it be a rolled R or a softer R?

7. And what if there is an R in the middle of a word (as in *fuerte*)? Should it be a rolled R or a softer R?

8. How would you pronounce *guerra*? And what about *gorila*?

9. In Spanish, does the verb usually come before or after the subject?

10. Can a pronoun be the subject of a sentence?

11. True or false: In Spanish, you should always have an overt subject.

12. In Spanish, does the order of a statement need to change to turn it into a question?

13. True or false: The adjectives in Spanish usually go after the noun they modify.

14. True or false: The Spanish word for the color orange is *amarillo.*

15. A chessboard is usually of which two colors?

    a. Rojo y azul

    b. Gris y verde

    c. Blanco y negro

16. In Spanish, what is usually the color of strawberries?

17. What number comes after *tres?*

18. And what number comes before *ocho?*

19. How many people are there in Sarah's family if she has two brothers, a sister, a mother, and a father? (Answer in Spanish!)

Chapter 2: Meeting New People

¡Bienvenidos al capítulo 2!

It's Sarah here, again! Julio and I have just arrived in Barcelona. For this holiday, I want to make friends with Julio's friends and meet some new people. However, there's that awful language barrier. Luckily, I have Julio.

Julio's father, Ernesto, came to pick us up at the airport. Julio taught me how to meet new people so that I can introduce myself to his father. To do so, we practiced the following conversation a few times:

○ Buenos días. ¿Cómo te llamas?	○ Good morning. What's your name?
● Hola, me llamo Sarah. ¿Y tú?	● Hello, my name is Sarah. And yours?
○ Yo soy Julio. ¿De dónde eres?	○ I'm Julio. Where are you from?
● Soy estadounidense. ¿Y tú de dónde eres?	● I'm American. And where are you from?

○ Soy de aquí, de Barcelona. ¿Y a qué te dedicas?	○ I'm from here, from Barcelona. And what do you do for a living?
● Soy contadora. ¿Y tú?	● I'm an accountant. And you?
○ Yo soy profesor de español. ¿Cuántos años tienes?	○ I'm a Spanish teacher. How old are you?
● Treinta y cuatro. ¿Y tú?	● Thirty four. And you?
○ Yo tengo treinta y ocho. Debo irme. Fue un placer conocerte.	○ I'm thirty eight. I have to go. It was a pleasure to meet you.
● ¡Gracias e igualmente!	● Thank you, you too!

Conversations like this one allowed me to learn a lot of basic phrases and expressions to meet new people. So I felt a bit more confident when Ernesto came to pick us up. The first bit of the conversation went something like this:

● ¡Hola, Ernesto! Es un placer conocerte.	● Hello, Ernesto!
○ ¡Hola! ¿Eres Sarah, verdad?	○ Hello! You are Sarah, right?
● Sí, así es.	● Yes, that's right.
○ ¿Cómo estás?	○ How are you?
● Muy bien, gracias.	● Very well, thank you.

Then, after we'd put our suitcases in the trunk and started on our way to Julio's home, we continued our conversation:

o Sarah, ¿de dónde vienes?	o Sarah, where are you from?
• De Estados Unidos. Soy estadounidense.	• From the United States. I'm American.
o ¡Ah! ¿Es lindo donde vives?	o Oh! Is it nice where you live?
• Sí, claro. A mí me encanta.	• Yes, sure. I love it.
o Algún día debemos ir a visitar a Julio. ¿Cuántos años tienes?	o Someday we have to go visit Julio. How old are you?
• Tengo treinta y dos años. ¿Y tú?	• I'm thirty two. And you?
o Yo tengo ochenta y cuatro años. Pero luzco más joven ¿verdad?	o I'm eighty four. But I look younger, don't I?

Julio is now going to teach you everything he taught me. Are you ready to meet new people? *¡Vamos!*

Greetings and farewells

Hey! It's Julio again. To meet new people, we first need to greet them, right? Here's a list of common ways to greet someone in Spanish (with their pronunciation!)

- *Hola*: It is the standard way of saying "hello." It is pronounced /oḷä/
- *Buen día*: It is another way of saying hello that can be used throughout the day. It is pronounced /βueṇ diä/
- *Buenos días*: This one is used to greet only during the morning, until around midday. It is pronounced /βueṇoṣ diäs/

- *Buenas tardes*: It is only used during the afternoon, from midday until around sundown, which is at different times depending on the season and the country. It is pronounced /βueṇäs tärde̞s/

- *Buenas noches*: It is only used during the night and can be used to say hello or even to say goodbye when we're about to go to bed. It is pronounced /βueṇäs no̞tʃe̞s/

- *¿Cómo estás?*: It means "How are you?" but it can also be used to greet someone. It is pronounced /ko̞mo̞ e̞stäs/

Now, let's see some options to say goodbye as well:

- *Adiós*: This is the standard way of saying goodbye in most Spanish-speaking countries. It is pronounced /ädio̞s/

- *Chao*: In some countries with great Italian influence, people use *chao* or *chau* even more than *adiós*. It is pronounced /tʃäo̞/ or /tʃäü/.

- *Nos vemos*: We can also use *nos vemos* to say goodbye. It is similar to the English "see you!" and it is pronounced /no̞s be̞mo̞s/.

- *Hasta luego*: This way of saying goodbye means "see you later!" but it is used even if you don't have plans to see that person later. You can also change the *luego* with the time or day you plan to see that person, for example, *hasta mañana* ("see you tomorrow!").

Subject Pronouns

Now it's time to talk about subject pronouns, which we've already discussed before! So, let's refresh your memory and delve deeper into this topic.

Spanish personal pronouns can be used to replace nouns in the subject when the people in the conversation know who we're talking about. In Spanish, the personal pronouns are:

- First-person singular: *yo* ("I")
- Second-person singular: *tú* / *usted* ("you")
- Third-person singular: *él* / *ella* ("he" / "she")
- First-person plural: *nosotros* / *nosotras* ("we")

- Second-person plural: *vosotros / vosotras / ustedes* ("you")
- Third-person plural: *ellos / ellas* ("they")

Keep in mind that there are two options in the second-person singular. *Usted* is the formal version of *tú,* and it is used for formal situations, with elderly people, or with people you have just met for the first time.

I want to draw your attention to the second-person plural, in which you will find that there are three options. *Ustedes* is mostly used in Latin American countries, while *vosotros* and *vosotras* are used mainly in Spain. And you may be wondering what the differences are between *vosotros* and *vosotras;* I'll explain in the following section.

Gender and Number

Gender is one of the aspects in which Spanish and English greatly differ. In Spanish, gender is not only for people, but also for *things.* Every noun has a gender that can be either feminine or masculine.

Since pronouns are used in the place of nouns, they also have a gender, which is why we saw that many of the pronouns from the table had two options. Generally speaking, the nouns (or, in this case, pronouns) that end in *A* are usually feminine, while those that end in *O* are usually masculine.

As for number, we've been indirectly talking about number in the previous section. When we talk about the number of nouns (or pronouns like in the previous section), we're referring to whether they are singular or plural.

In Spanish, we pluralize nouns in a similar way to English: by adding *-S, -ES,* or *-CES* at the end. For example, *libro* ("book") turns into *libros,* and *pez* ("fish") turns into *peces.* Here's the rule for pluralization in Spanish:

- If the singular form ends in a vowel, you must add an *-s* at the end.
  - Examples: *mesa → mesas, casa → casas, mono → monos, pelota → pelotas*

- If the singular form ends in a consonant or with a stressed vowel, you must add -*es* at the end.
  - Examples: *ataúd → ataúdes, iglú → iglúes, rey → reyes, pared → paredes*
- If the singular form ends with Z, you must add -*ces* at the end.
  - Examples: *pez → peces, voz → voces, nuez → nueces, lápiz → lápices*

At this point, I should warn you that the gender and number of nouns is a bit more complicated than what we've seen so far because, in Spanish, gender and number don't only affect nouns, but also articles, verbs, and adjectives. This is what we call *concordancia* ("agreement"). Articles and adjectives should always agree in gender and number with the nouns they modify, and verbs should always agree in number with the nouns they modify. So, for instance, if we want to say "the house is pretty" in Spanish and we know that *casa* ("house") is a feminine word, we would say <u>la</u> *casa* <u>es</u> *lind<u>a</u>*. However, if we want to say "the buildings are pretty" and we know that *edificio* ("building") is a masculine word, we would say <u>los</u> *edificios* <u>son</u> *lind<u>os</u>*.

The verb "to be"

As a last grammar topic in this chapter, and before we get into the vocabulary, I'd like to tell you about the conjugation of the verb "to be" in Spanish. We've just seen an example of it in use, but we should remember that, in Spanish, the verb "to be" can either mean *ser* or *estar*. Yes, another complicated Spanish thing!

To sum it up, *ser* is used for permanent or long-lasting states, for example, *Soy de París* ("I'm from Paris"). However, *estar* is for temporary states, for example, *Estoy en París* ("I'm in Paris").

These two verbs are irregular verbs in Spanish and, in the present form, are conjugated in the following way:

	SER	ESTAR
1st person singular: *yo*	*soy*	*estoy*
2nd person singular: *tú*	*eres*	*estás*
3rd person singular: *él / ella / usted*	*es*	*está*
1st person plural: *nosotros / nosotras*	*somos*	*estamos*
2nd person plural: *vosotros / vosotras*	*sois*	*estáis*
3rd person plural: *ellos / ellas / ustedes*	*son*	*están*

You may have noticed that I told you *ustedes* was another form of the second person plural, but in the chart above, it shows up in the *third* person plural box.

I don't mean to confuse you (and I didn't make a mistake!) *Ustedes* is, indeed, a form of the second person plural, but its conjugation is always the same as the third person plural. Keep this in mind for future reference!

And you might also be wondering what *usted* means; it is the formal version of the second-person singular. But, you can see that it is grouped with the third person singular in the previous table because it is conjugated like the third person – exactly like with *ustedes*, but in the singular.

Asking Simple Questions

Now it's time to get down to business. In this section, we'll see some useful phrases that you might ask or be asked when meeting people!

- *¿Cómo te llamas?* means "What's your name?"
- *¿Cuál es tu apellido?* means "What's your last name?"
- *¿De dónde eres?* means "Where are you from?"
- *¿Cuántos años tienes?* means "How old are you?"
- *¿Cuál es tu nacionalidad?* means "What's your nationality?"

And you may be wondering how to answer some of these questions, so we'll see that in the following section.

Introducing ourselves

Let's tackle this question by question.

¿Cómo te llamas? can be answered in three ways. The first one is by saying *Me llamo...* followed by your name. For example: *Me llamo Julio* or *Me llamo Beatriz.*

The second way is to say *Mi nombre es...* followed by your name, which is the equivalent of "My name is..." Examples of this could be: *Mi nombre es Pedro* or *Mi nombre es Isabel.*

The third way includes a verb we've already seen, *ser.* Since how you're called is supposed to be a permanent state, we use *ser* the way we use "I am" in English. For example: *Soy Camilo* or *Soy Paula.*

If we are asked for our last name, we can simply answer with our last name or use the verb *ser* in this way: *Es Fernández* or *Es García.*

So far, so good, right?

To answer the question *¿De dónde eres?*, we could use the phrase *Soy de...* followed by your country. For example: *Soy de Alemania* ("I'm from Germany ") or *Soy de Francia* ("I'm from France").

To answer *¿Cuántos años tienes?* You say *tengo...* followed by your age and then the word *años.* But I haven't taught you numbers over 10, right? No worries; that section is right after this one! Keep in mind that while in English we use the verb "to be" when saying our age, in Spanish we can't use the verbs *ser* or *estar; instead, we* should always use *tengo,* which is the first person singular of the verb *tener.* For example: *Tengo treinta y cuatro años* or *Tengo* *quince años.*

If someone asks you what your nationality is, the only way to answer is to use the verb *ser*. For example: *Soy portugués* ("I'm Portuguese") and *Soy chilena ("I'm Chilean")*. For this answer, you should always remember that the noun should always agree in gender and number with you! So, if you're a woman and you're with your sister, you could answer *Somos venezolanas ("We are Venezuelan")*. But if I were alone, I would answer *Soy español ("I'm Spaniard")*. This response could also be used to answer the question *¿De dónde eres?* ("Where are you from?") If you want to know what your country and nationality are called in Spanish, I've made a list for you after the numbers section!

Numbers over 20

If someone asks for your age, you probably will need to know numbers higher than 20 to be able to answer, right? Well, in this first list, you'll see what numbers 20 to 29 are called in Spanish.

20.	*veinte*
21.	*veintiuno*
22.	*veintidós*
23.	*veintitrés*
24.	*veinticuatro*
25.	*veinticinco*
26.	*veintiséis*
27.	*veintisiete*
28.	*veintiocho*
29.	*veintinueve*

Now, in this second list, you can find the tens from 30 to 100:

30.	*treinta*
40.	*cuarenta*
50.	*cincuenta*
60.	*sesenta*
70.	*setenta*
80.	*ochenta*
90.	*noventa*

100.   cien

From 31 to 99, we can form the rest of the numbers that aren't on the list by adding *y* and the number we need. For example, to form the number 64, we just need to say *sesenta y cuatro*. And if we wanted to say 82, we would say *ochenta y cuatro*.

Countries and nationalities

To answer the questions about where you come from and your nationality, you need to know some countries and nationalities, so here's a list that will come in handy. Of course, it isn't a complete list of all the countries, but you can always search for others and complete the list. We'll start with my country and Sarah's!

You should also bear in mind that, unlike in English, in Spanish, nationalities are not capitalized and should agree in gender and number with the person we are talking about (whether it is ourselves or someone else).

Countries	Nationalities
Estados Unidos United States	*estadounidense*
España Spain	*español*
México Mexico	*mexicano*
Inglaterra England	*inglés*
Australia Australia	*australiano*
Francia France	*francés*

Colombia Colombia	*colombiano*
Perú Peru	*peruano*
China China	*chino*
Brasil Brazil	*brasilero*
Chile Chile	*chileno*
Argentina Argentina	*argentino*
Guatemala Guatemala	*guatemalteco*
Venezuela Venezuela	*venezolano*
Cuba Cuba	*cubano*
Sudáfrica South Africa	*sudafricano*
Alemania Germany	*alemán*

Italia Italy	*italiano*
Egipto Egypt	*egipcio*
Grecia Greece	*griego*

Exercises

1. Which of these expressions is not used to greet someone?
    a. Nos vemos
    b. Hola
    c. Buen día

2. If we want to say goodbye to someone and tell them that we'll see them tomorrow, how would we say it?
    a. Chao mañana
    b. Hasta luego
    c. Hasta mañana

3. Which of these is not a feminine pronoun?
    a. ellos
    b. ella
    c. vosotras

4. What is the first person masculine plural pronoun?
    a. tú
    b. nosotros
    c. ellos

5. Usually, masculine nouns end in what letter?

6. Considering the rules of pluralization in Spanish. What would be the plural forms of *mano, vaso* and *silla*?

7. What is the plural form of *luz?*

    a. lus

    b. luzes

    c. luces

8. In Spanish, many words can reflect gender. Which of these doesn't?

    a. verbs

    b. articles

    c. adjectives

9. True or false: *Estar* is used for temporary states.

10. True or false: *Ustedes* is the pronoun of the 3rd person plural, so it's conjugated in the same way as *ellos* and *ellas.*

11. What are the conjugations of *ser* and *estar* in the first person singular?

12. Which of these sentences meaning "She is happy" is correct?

    a. Ella es contentos

    b. Ella está contento

    c. Ella está contenta

13. Which one is a possible answer to the question ¿*Cómo te llamas?*?

    a. Soy Julio

    b. Estoy Julio

    c. Llamo me Julio

14. Which one is a possible answer to the question ¿*Cuál es tu apellido?*?

    a. Soy Sánchez

    b. Estoy Sánchez

    c. Es Sánchez

15. Which one is a possible answer to the question ¿*De dónde eres?*?

    a. Soy de España

    b. Estoy España

c. Es España

16. Which one is a possible answer to the question ¿*Cuántos años tienes?*?

    a. Soy veinte años

    b. Tengo veinte años

    c. Los veinte años

17. Which one is a possible answer to the question ¿*Cuál es tu nacionalidad?*?

    a. Francia

    b. Estoy francés

    c. Soy francés

18. How do you form the number thirty-seven in Spanish?

19. How do you form the number twenty-nine in Spanish?

20. What is the feminine form of German in Spanish?

Chapter 3: Checking Into Your Room

Hello – Sarah here. After visiting Julio's family in Barcelona, we took the train to Bilbao, the capital of the Basque Country. The Basque Country is an autonomous community in northwest Spain. In Spanish, the region is known as *País Vasco* or *Euskadi*. I wanted to visit it because it has its own language, a rich culinary tradition (mainly *pintxos* or small snacks of lamb, cured meats, salt cod, and cheese), and a beautiful geographic landscape (including the coast of the Atlantic Ocean and the mountains near the border with France). Besides, I wanted to take the opportunity to learn some more Spanish!

However, when we were on the train, we realized that we hadn't considered that we were going to Bilbao during the Semana Grande de Bilbao, the main city festivities. That's why we had a little trouble getting in touch with a hotel that had rooms available. When we finally got one, I asked Julio to put the phone on speaker, so I could listen to the conversation and learn some useful phrases.

○ Buenos días, se comunicó con el Hotel Conde Duque de Bilbao, mi nombre es Carlos, ¿en qué puedo ayudarle?	○ Good morning, you are talking with the Hotel Conde Duque in Bilbao, my name is Carlos, how can I help you?
● Buenos días, quería reservar una habitación para hoy.	● Good morning, I wanted to book a room for today.
○ ¿Para cuántas personas?	○ For how many people?
● Para dos personas, con dos camas y baño completo, por favor.	● For two people, with two beds and a bathroom, please.
○ Muy bien, ¿y cuántas noches van a quedarse?	○ Very well, and how many nights are you going to stay?
● Nos quedaremos tres noches.	● We'll stay three nights.
○ Vale. ¿Quieren incluir el desayuno? Se sirve en el salón comedor, con vistas a la Ría de Bilbao.	○ Good. Do you want to include breakfast? It's served in the dining room, with a view of the Estuary of Bilbao.
● Pues sí, con desayuno incluido, por favor.	● Okay, yes, with breakfast included, please.
○ ¿Podría decirme los nombres de los dos huéspedes, por favor?	○ Could you tell me the names of the two guests, please?

• Claro, yo soy Julio Sánchez y mi acompañante es Sarah Williams.	• Sure, I'm Julio Sánchez, and my companion is Sarah Williams.
○ De acuerdo, a partir de las 2 de la tarde estará lista la habitación, señor Sánchez.	○ Very well, from 2 p.m. the room will be ready.
• Muy amable, hasta luego.	• Thank you, see you later.

We arrived at the train station and decided to walk to the hotel, which was only ten minutes away. When we crossed the Ría de Bilbao, an estuary, we caught a glimpse of the Guggenheim Museum. The state-of-the-art building is home to a museum of modern and contemporary art, and it's one of the landmarks of Bilbao. I really wanted to visit it. But first, we had to check in at our hotel; I paid attention to Julio's conversation with the receptionist.

○ Buenas tardes, tenemos una reserva.	○ Good afternoon. We have a booking.
• Buenas tardes, bienvenidos. ¿A nombre de quién está la reserva?	• Good afternoon, wellcome. Under which name is the booking?
○ La reserva está a nombre de Julio Sánchez y Sarah Williams.	○ The booking is under the names Julio Sánchez and Sarah Williams.
• Deme un momento... Aquí está. Una habitación doble, con baño completo y	• One moment, please... Here it is. A double room with bathroom, and breakfast included, right?

desayuno incluido, ¿verdad?	
○ Sí, es correcto.	○ Yes, it's correct.
● Vale. El precio por las tres noches es de 250€. ¿Cómo desea abonar? ¿Con tarjeta o en efectivo?	● Very well. The price for the three nights is 250€. How would you like to pay? Card or cash?
○ En efectivo, si es posible.	○ Cash, if that's okay.
● Claro, por supuesto. Bien, aquí tienen la llave de la habitación. La habitación se encuentra en el tercer piso. Es la habitación 305. Pueden tomar el ascensor que está a la derecha. También pueden subir por las escaleras, que se encuentran al final del pasillo. ¿Tienen alguna otra pregunta?	● Yes, of course. Very well, here's the key to the room. The room is on the third floor. It's room 305. You can take the elevator that's on your right. You can also use the stairs, which are at the end of the corridor. Do you have any other questions?
○ No, por ahora no. Muchas gracias.	○ No, not right now. Thank you very much.

After listening to that conversation, I had a lot of questions! Luckily, Julio was able to help me with all of them.

Definite/Indefinite Articles

The first question Sarah asked me when we got to our room in Bilbao was about something I said. She wanted to know what did *una* mean in *Tenemos una reserva ("We have a booking")*, so I took the chance to talk about definite and indefinite articles in Spanish.

Similar to English, nouns in Spanish are often preceded by a definite or indefinite article. Spanish has four variations of the definite article, whereas English uses only "the." Like many other words in Spanish, the definite article changes according to the gender and the number of single or plural nature of the noun that comes after it.

> Before masculine singular nouns, we use *el*: *¿Quieren incluir el desayuno? ("Do you want to include breakfast?")*

> Before feminine singular nouns, we use *la*: *La reserva está a nombre de Julio Sánchez y Sarah Williams* ("The booking is under the names Julio Sánchez and Sarah Williams.")

> Before masculine plural nouns, we use *los*: *¿Podría decirme los nombres de los dos huéspedes, por favor?* ("Could you tell me the names of the two guests, please?")

> Before feminine plural nouns, we use *las*: *También pueden subir por las escaleras ("You can also use the stairs.")*

Whereas English has "a," "an," and "some," Spanish also has four indefinite articles that change depending on the gender and number of the noun they are modifying.

> Before singular masculine nouns, we use *un*: *Conseguimos un hotel muy bonito ("We found a really nice hotel.")*

> Before singular feminine nouns, we use *una*: *Buenas tardes, tenemos una reserva ("Good afternoon, we have a booking.")*

> Before plural masculine nouns, we use *unos*: *En Bilbao nos tocaron unos días espléndidos ("In Bilbao we had some splendid days.")*

Before plural feminine nouns, we use *unas*: *En el desayuno servían unas tortas deliciosas ("For breakfast they served delicious cakes.")*

And, to make things a little bit trickier, Spanish also has the neuter article *lo*. We use this gender-free article in front of adjectives to transform them into abstract nouns or talk about a *quality*. In English, we use "thing" or "part" when we want to do this. Let's take a look at this example: *Lo mejor del hotel es la ubicación ("The best thing of the hotel was the location.")*

	Masculine		Feminine	
	Singular	Plural	Singular	Plural
Definite	*El*	*Los*	*La*	*Las*
Indefinite	*Un*	*Unos*	*Una*	*Unas*
Neuter	*Lo*			

Booking a Room

I paid attention while Julio was booking the room and was able to write down these useful phrases. Then, he added some more. Next time we check into a hotel, I will do the talking!

Asking for a room:

- *Quería reservar una habitación para esta noche*: I want to book a room for tonight.

- *¿Tiene habitaciones disponibles?*: Do you have any rooms available?

- *Quiero una habitación simple*: I want a single room

- *Me gustaría una habitación con baño privado*: I'd like a room with a private bathroom.

Asking about the price:

- *¿Cuál es el precio de una habitación doble?*: What's the price for a double room?

- *¿Tiene una opción más económica?*: Do you have a cheaper option?

- *¿Puedo pagar en efectivo?*: Can I pay with cash?

- *Solo tengo tarjeta de crédito*: I only have credit card

Asking about specific features:

- *Me gustaría una habitación con vista*: I would like a room with a view.

- *¿El desayuno está incluido?*: Is breakfast included?

- *¿A qué hora se sirve el desayuno?*: At what time is breakfast served?

- *¿Ofrecen servicios de traslado al aeropuerto?*: Do you offer airport transfer service?

- *¿El hotel tiene Wi Fi?*: Does the hotel have wifi?

- *¿Puedo ver la habitación?*: Can I see the room?

Yes/No Questions

Something that puzzled Sarah about *written* Spanish was the upside-down question mark, or, as we call it, the opening question mark, which has a very important function. We use the opening and closing question marks (and exclamation marks, as well) in writing to distinguish questions from affirmative statements (or to show exuberance or emphasis, in the case of exclamation points). In speaking, we mark the difference simply with our intonation.

Let's take a closer look at some questions from the previous section.

¿El desayuno está incluido? ("Is breakfast included?") has the same word order as *El desayuno está incluido* ("Breakfast is included"). The only difference is the question marks. The same happens with *¿El hotel tiene Wi-Fi?* ("Does the hotel have wifi?"), which is written in the same order as *El hotel tiene Wi Fi* ("The hotel has wifi.") So, forming yes/no questions in *written* Spanish is

not such a difficult task.

Prepositions of Place

One of the biggest challenges for non-natives are prepositions. But don't worry. We'll make it simple and, for now, we'll focus on prepositions of place. Let's use this short text Sarah wrote – describing our first day walking in Bilbao – to learn about prepositions of place.

Empezamos el recorrido en el hotel.	We started the walk at the hotel.
Primero caminamos por las calles de alrededor.	First, we walked through the surrounding streets.
Después, nos dirigimos al museo.	After that, we went to the museum.
A la derecha del museo está la Ría.	To the right of the museum is the estuary.
Cerca de ahí, después de un puente, nos topamos con la Plaza Nueva Bilbao.	Near there, after a bridge, we came to Plaza Nueva Bilbao.
Dentro de la plaza, hay un monumento.	Inside the square, there's a monument.
Encima del monumento hay muchas palomas.	On top of the monument, there are many pigeons.
Volvimos caminando hacia el hotel.	We walked back to the hotel.

- *en* means "in"
- *alrededor* means "about"
- *a* means "to," "by" or "at"

- *a la derecha de* means "to the right of"
- *cerca de* means "near to"
- *después de* means "after"
- *dentro de* means "in," "inside" or "within"
- *encima de* means "on top of"
- *hacia* means "toward"

Asking for the Room Number

Something funny happened while Sarah and I were in Bilbao. When we returned to the hotel after our first day walking around the city, we had forgotten our room number! However, as the saying goes, "success is where preparation and opportunity meet," so we took the opportunity to test Sarah's preparation, and she was the one in charge of asking for our room number.

○ Hola, buenas noches.	○ Hello, good evening.
● Buenas noches, señorita, ¿en qué la puedo ayudar?	● Good evening, miss, how can I help you?
○ Perdón que lo moleste, pero mi amigo y yo olvidamos en qué habitación estamos alojados.	○ I'm sorry to bother you, but my friend and I forgot which room we are staying in.
● No se preocupe, es bastante común. ¿Podría decirme sus nombres?	● Don't worry, it's pretty common. Could you tell me your names?
○ Sí, yo me llamo Sarah Williams y él se llama Julio Sánchez.	○ Yes, my name is Sarah Williams and his name is Julio Sánchez.
● Muy bien, señorita Williams, su habitación es la 305, en el tercer piso.	● Very well, miss Williams, your room is room 305, on the third floor.

o ¡305! Claro, ahora que lo dice me suena. Muchas gracias.	o ¡305! Of course, now you say it, it rings a bell. Thank you.
• De nada, buenas noches.	• You are welcome, good night.

Parts of a House

During my short time in Spain, I realized that Spanish houses are very similar to those in the States. For example, Ernesto's house in Barcelona had all of these parts:

- *la puerta principal*, which is the front door
- *la sala*, which is the living room
- *el comedor*, which is the dining-room
- *la cocina*, which is the kitchen
- *el trastero*, which is the storage room
- *el baño*, which is the bathroom
- *la habitación/dormitorio*, which is the bedroom
- *la chimenea*, which is the fireplace
- *la escalera*, which is the stairs
- *las ventanas*, which are the windows
- *el pasillo*, which is the hallway
- *el jardín*, which is the garden
- *el ático*, which is the attic
- *el sótano*, which is the basement

Objects in the House

While I walked around Ernesto's house in Barcelona, I asked Julio the names of all the objects I saw. Afterward, he helped me, and together we made the following vocabulary list.

In the kitchen:

- *el fregadero* is the sink
- *el grifo* is the faucet
- *la estufa* is the stove
- *el horno* is the oven

- *el refrigerador* is the refrigerator
- *el congelador* is the freezer
- *el lavaplatos* is the dishwasher
- *los electrodomésticos* are the appliances
- *la encimera* is the counter
- *la despensa* is the pantry
- *la alacena* is the cupboard

In the living room:

- *la silla* is the chair
- *el sillón* is the armchair
- *el reloj* is the clock
- *la mesita* is coffee table
- *la lámpara* is the lamp
- *el florero* is the vase
- *la alfombra* is the carpet

In the bedroom:

- *la cama* is the bed
- *el tapete* is the rug
- *la lamparilla* is the nightlight
- *las cortinas* are the curtains
- *el armario* is the closet
- *la cómoda* is the dresser
- *el despertador* is the alarm clock

In the bathroom:

- *la toalla* is the towel
- *el espejo* is the mirror
- *la pasta de dientes* is the toothpaste
- *el cepillo de dientes* is the toothbrush
- *el jabón* is the soap
- *el peine* is the comb
- *el cepillo* is the brush

- *la maquinilla de afeitar* is the razor
- *la crema de afeitar* is the shaving cream
- *el maquillaje* is the makeup

Describing the Room

In the hotel room, I decided to write a short text describing the room to practice the vocabulary I had learned in Barcelona:

La habitación tiene dos camas individuales.	There are two single beds.
Las camas tienen sábanas y edredones de color blanco.	The beds have white sheets and quilts.
A los lados de las camas hay dos mesitas de luz y dos lamparillas.	To the sides of the beds there are two night stands with dos lamps.
Detrás de las camas, en el centro de la pared, hay una pintura de un tulipán.	Behind the beds, in the middle of the wall, there's a picture of a tulip.
Al costado de la cama que está a la derecha, hay una ventana.	To the side of the bed that's to the right, there's a window.
La ventana tiene cortinas oscuras con lunares claros.	The window has dark curtains with light dots.
Las cortinas están corridas.	The curtains are drawn.
Del otro lado de la ventana, al lado de la cama de la izquierda, hay una mesa redonda y un sofá.	On the other side of the window, next to the bed that's to the left, there's a round table and a sofa.

Hotel room.

Exercises

Let's see how much you've learned during our time in Bilbao!

1. How many definite articles are there in Spanish?
    a. Just one
    b. Four
    c. Two
2. What characteristics of the noun define which definite article to use?
3. Can you name the definite articles in Spanish?
4. True or false: Spanish has six indefinite articles.
5. Can you name the Spanish indefinite articles?
6. Before *flor*, a singular, feminine noun, which of these indefinite articles would you use?
    a. Unas
    b. Un
    c. Una

7. Before *ríos*, a plural masculine noun, which of these definite articles would you use?

    a. Los

    b. Las

    c. El

8. At a hotel front desk, how would you ask for a single room for the night?

9. True or false: *habitación doble* is a room for two people.

10. Can you name the means of payment mentioned in the chapter?

11. True or false: To distinguish questions from affirmative sentences in written Spanish, we use ONLY the opening question mark.

12. How do you tell the difference between questions and affirmative sentences when speaking?

13. If you want to say something is *in* or *inside* something else, which of the following prepositions of place would you use?

    a. Encima de

    b. Hacia

    c. En

14. True or false: The preposition *a* can mean "to," "by" and "at."

15. Can you name the parts of the house that you remember?

16. Cross the odd one out:

    a. La cocina

    b. El dormitorio

    c. El baño

    d. El jarrón

    e. La sala

17. Which of these objects would you NOT find in a kitchen?

    a. Un horno

    b. Una toalla

    c. Un electrodoméstico

d.　Un grifo

18. Can you name four objects normally found in a bedroom?

19. In which room do you think you can find *un espejo?* (It could be more than one room)

20. In which room do you think you can find *una cama?* (It could be more than one room)

Chapter 4: Going Shopping

Hi! Julio here. After a few lovely days in Bilbao, I took Sarah to the amazing community of Galicia. We had a 10-hour train journey to Santiago de Compostela, Galicia's capital city, so I took advantage of that time to tell her a bit more about this autonomous community. Galicia is located in the far north western corner of Spain, just above Portugal, with the Atlantic Ocean to the west and the Cantabrian Sea to the north. Because of this, the community is famous for its coasts, which alternate between *rías* (estuaries) and beaches. Inland Galicia is full of hills and low mountains, and it's very green because the weather is humid and rainy.

A curious thing about Galicia is that, apart from Spanish, Portuguese and Galician are also spoken in the region. The latter is a romance language closely related to Portuguese, and it's spoken daily by half the population of Galicia. The *Camino de Santiago* ("Way of St James") is also worth noting. It's a trail network that takes pilgrims to the St. James shrine, located in the cathedral of Santiago de Compostela. This brings hundreds of thousands of travelers from all over the world to the region each year.

Besides its beautiful scenery and vibrant culture, another reason I wanted to take Sarah to Galicia is its delicious cuisine, which includes shellfish, *empanadas* (turnovers with savory filling), *pulpo a la gallega* (octopus cooked the Galician way), and *orujo* liquor (distilled from grape remains). Besides, there are also several typical guisados (stews) because of the link with de Celtic culture.

In Galicia, we visited Santiago, La Coruña, a port city with beaches, museums, and monuments, and Finisterre, the farthest western point in Spain.

Demonstrative Pronouns and Articles

I was glad Julio wanted to take me to Galicia. Back home, my mom and dad are avid hikers. One of their dreams is to one day walk the *Camino de Santiago*. So, once I was in Santiago de Compostela, the ultimate mecca for hikers and pilgrims, I wanted to buy lots of presents for them. That's why I asked Julio to take me to a souvenir shop. There, I was able to buy a t-shirt for my mom, all by myself!

• ¡Buenos días! ¿En qué puedo ayudarla?	• Good morning! How can I help you?
○ Hola, me gustaría comprar una camiseta.	○ Hello, I'd like to buy a t-shirt.
• Por supuesto. ¿De niño, de hombre o de mujer?	• Very well. For kids, men or women?
○ Quiero una camiseta de mujer.	○ I want a woman's t-shirt.
• ¿De qué talla la quiere?	• In which size do you want it?
○ La quiero en talla mediana.	○ I want it in medium size.
• Muy bien, tenemos camisetas de mujer en talla mediana de color rosado, amarillo y celeste. ¿De qué color le gusta?	• Great, we have women's t-shirts of medium size in pink, yellow and light blue. Which color do you like?

○ Me gustaría de color rosado. Y con el logo del Camino de Santiago, como aquella camiseta que está allí.	○ I'd like it in pink. And with the logo of the Camino de Santiago, like that t-shirt over there.
● Esa no la tengo en rosado. ¿Qué le parece esta, que tiene el logo en la espalda?	● That one I don't have in pink. What do you think about this one, with the logo on the back?
○ Vale, llevo esa. ¿Cuánto cuesta?	○ Okay, I'll take that one. How much is it?
● La camiseta cuesta 10€. ¿Se la envuelvo para regalo?	● The t-shirt is 10€. Do you want it wrapped?
○ Sí, por favor.	○ Yes, please
● Aquí tiene. ¡Gracias por su compra! Adiós.	● Here you are. Thank you for your purchase! Goodbye.

And, as always, Julio took the chance to teach me something new about Spanish!

Demonstrative pronouns are words used instead of nouns to point at people or things, for example, *Esa no la tengo en rosado ("That one I don't have in pink.")* When they accompany the noun, they function as articles; for example, *aquella camiseta que está allí ("that t-shirt over there.")*

The demonstrative pronouns in English are "this," "that," "these," and "those." In Spanish, however, we have quite a few more. To choose from the list of 15 Spanish demonstrative pronouns, we need to consider the gender, the number, and the distance from the speaker and the addressee of the noun it's replacing.

	Masculine		Feminine		Neuter
	Singular	Plural	Singular	Plural	Singular
Object close to the speaker	esto	estos	esta	estas	esto
Object close to the addressee	ese	eso	esa	esas	eso
Object far from both	aquel	aquellos	aquella	aquellas	aquello

Speaking about the Price of a Product

Since Sarah wanted to do some shopping in Santiago de Compostela, I taught her some useful phrases to ask for prices and, also, what to expect as an answer:

Asking for prices

- *¿Cuánto cuesta/sale/vale esto?*: How much is this?
- *¿Cuánto cuestan/salen/valen esos?*: How much are those?
- *¿Qué precio tiene?*: What's the price?
- *¿Cuál es el precio?*: What's the price?
- *¿A qué precio está?*: What's the price?
- *¿Qué vale?*: How much?
- *¿Cuánto es?*: How much is it?

Telling prices

- *El precio de eso son 5€*: The price of that is 5€.
- *Vale/cuesta/sale 20€*: It's 20€.
- *Es 1€*: It's 1€.
- *Son 15€*: It's 15€.

Interrogative Pronouns/"W" questions (Why, What, Who, etc.)

I used different interrogative pronouns in the questions I taught Sarah about asking prices in stores. Let's take a look at them.

- *qué* is used in the same way as English "what": *¿Qué precio tiene este pastel?* ("What is the price of this cake?").

- *por qué* is similar to English "why": *¿Por qué están tan caros los tomates?* ("Why are tomatoes so expensive?").

- *cuál* and *cuáles* are the singular and plural equivalents of English "which": *¿Cuál prefieres, el de atún o el de pollo?* ("Which one do you want, the tuna or the chicken one?").

- *quién* and *quiénes* are the singular and plural equivalents of "who": *¿Quién quiere lechuga?* ("Who wants lettuce?").

- *cuánto* and *cuánta* are the masculine and feminine equivalents of "how much": *¿Cuánto pan compro?* ("How much bread should I buy").

- *cuántos* and *cuántas* are the masculine and feminine equivalents of "how many": *¿Cuántas piñas desea?* ("How many pineapples do you want?").

- *dónde* is used in the same way as English "where": *¿Dónde está el arroz en esta tienda?* ("Where is the rice in this store").

- *cómo* is used in the same way as "how": *¿Cómo se cocina el pulpo?* ("How is oct opus cooked?").

- *cuándo* is similar to English "when": *¿Cuándo abre el supermercado?* ("When does the supermarket open?").

Sarah noticed that all interrogative pronouns have a graphic accent and asked me about it. I explained to her that those words have more than one function in Spanish. So, to mark when they are being used as interrogative pronouns, they take an accent.

Asking for and Finding Products in a Store

In La Coruña, instead of staying in a hotel, Julio and I rented an apartment through Airbnb. Even though we love eating out, we also wanted to cook our own meals, and I wanted to learn how to make some typical Spanish dishes. That's why we went to the supermarket, where I had a few enriching conversations. The first one was with Julio:

• Julio, ¿sabes dónde puedo encontrar el jamón serrano?	• Julio, do you know where can I find the serrano ham?
○ Mmm, la verdad que no. ¿Te has fijado al lado del sector de panadería?	○ Mmm, actually, no. Have you looked next to the bakery sector?
• Pues sí, pero solo encontré lácteos. Había queso, leche, nata, yogur, pero nada de fiambres.	• Yes, but I only found dairy products. There's cheese, milk, cream, yogurt, but no cold cuts.
○ ¿Y al final del pasillo, antes de la verdulería?	○ And down the hall, before the greengrocers'?
• También he ido hasta allí y no he visto el jamón. Pero aproveché para coger algo de fruta y bastante verdura.	• I've also been there, but I haven't seen the ham. But I took the opportunity to grab some fruit and plenty of vegetables.
○ ¿Qué has cogido?	○ What have you grabbed?
• Tomates, lechuga, zanahoria, pepino, patatas, calabaza, manzanas, naranjas, fresas y ciruelas.	• Tomatoes, lettuce, carrots, cucumber, potatoes, pumpkin, apples, oranges, strawberries, and plums.
○ ¿No te parece que es mucho para un par de días?	○ Don't you think it's too much for a couple of days?

• Tienes razón, es demasiado, devolveré algunas cosas. ¿Tú que has cogido?	• You are right, it's too much, I'll put some things back.
○ Yo tengo los huevos y el aceite para hacer la tortilla de patatas. También conseguí arroz para la paella, pero no he encontrado los mariscos.	○ I have the eggs and the oil to make the potato tortilla. I also grabbed rice for the paella, but I haven't found the seafood.

The second dialogue I had was with one of the employees of the supermarket:

• Disculpe, ¿le puedo hacer una pregunta?	• Excuse me, can I ask you a question?
○ Buenas tardes. Sí, por supuesto, ¿en qué puedo ayudarla?	○ Good afternoon. Yes, of course, how can I help you?
• Me gustaría comprar jamón serrano.	• I'd like to buy serrano ham.
○ Los fiambres están en el pasillo 8, al lado de las galletas.	○ The cold cuts are in aisle 8, next to the cookies.
• Muchas gracias. ¿Hay pescadería en esta tienda?	• Thank you. Is there a fish market in this store?
○ Sí, claro. Está al final del pasillo 5, en la sección de productos frescos. ¿La puedo ayudar con algo más?	○ Yes, of course. It's at the end of aisle 5, in the fresh produce section. Is there anything else I can help you with?
• No, eso es todo. ¡Muchas gracias!	• No, that's all. Thank you!

Adverbs of Quantity

In the conversations she had in the supermarket, Sarah used a few adverbs of quantity: the words we use to answer "How much?" or "How many?" Here's a list of the most common ones:

- *mucho*: "many," "much," "a lot"
- *muy*: "very"
- *demasiado*: "too much"
- *bastante*: "enough," "quite"
- *algo*: "somewhat," "slightly," "a bit"
- *poco*: "little," "few"
- *nada*: "nothing," "at all"
- *más*: "more"
- *menos*: "less"
- *mucho más*: "a lot more"
- *tanto*: "so much"
- *tantos*: "so many"

Present Form of Regular Verbs

We've been traveling, and I've been studying Spanish for quite a while now. So I thought it was time to face one of my fears: the Spanish tenses. Luckily, Julio said we would start with the simplest one: the present simple. Here's his explanation.

We use the present simple to talk about what is generally true, for example: *Sarah vive en Estados Unidos* ("Sarah lives in the United States"). We also use this tense to talk about what is true at the moment, for example: *Estamos en España* ("We are in Spain"). Also, we use this tense to talk about what happens regularly, for example: *De lunes a viernes, doy clases de español en un colegio* ("Mondays through Fridays, I teach Spanish in a School").

Now, let's see how the verbs change to form this tense. The first thing you need to understand is that, in the infinitive form ("**to + verb**" - for example, "to talk," "to find" or "to fight"), all Spanish verbs end in -AR, -ER, or -IR. The verbs ending in -AR belong to the first conjugation, the verbs ending in -ER belong to the second conjugation, and the verbs ending in -IR belong to the third conjugation. The part that comes before those letters is called the verb's *root.*

Another important thing is that, just as in English, Spanish verbs can be regular or irregular. Within the regular ones, the ones that belong to the same conjugation undergo the same changes when we conjugate them.

Let's see how the regular verbs of the first conjugation change using the verb *amar* (to love). If we separate the verb into the root and ending, we are left with AM- (root) and -AR (ending). To conjugate the verb, we leave the root and change the ending like this:

For the present simple of the	first-person singular (yo)	we add -O	Yo amo
	first-person plural (nosotros / nosotras)	we add -AMOS	Nosotras / nosotros amamos
	second-person singular (tú)	we add -AS	Tú amas
	second-person singular (usted)	we add -A	Usted ama
	second-person plural (vosotros /vosotras)	we add -ÁIS	Vosotros / vosotras amáis
	second-person plural (ustedes)	we add -AN	Ustedes aman
	third-person singular (él / ella)	we add -A	Él / ella ama
	third-person plural (ellos / ellas)	we add -AN	Ellos / ellas aman

We follow the same logic with the regular verbs of the second conjugation. Let's see how we do it using *temer* (to fear).

For the present simple of the	first-person singular (yo)	we add -O	Yo temo
	first-person plural (nosotros / nosotras)	we add - EMOS	Nosotras / nosotros tememos
	second-person singular (tú)	we add -ES	Tú temes
	second-person singular (usted)	we add -E	Usted teme
	second-person plural (vosotros /vosotras)	we add -ÉIS	Vosotros / vosotras teméis
	second-person plural (ustedes)	we add -EN	Ustedes temen
	third-person singular (él / ella)	we add -E	Él / ella teme
	third-person plural (ellos / ellas)	we add -EN	Ellos / ellas temen

Lastly, let's see the same mechanism with *partir* (to leave) as an example of the third conjugation.

For the present simple of the	first-person singular (yo)	we add -O	Yo parto
	first-person plural (nosotros / nosotras)	we add - IMOS	Nosotras / nosotros partimos
	second-person singular (tú)	we add -ES	Tú partes
	second-person singular (usted)	we add -E	Usted parte

second-person plural (vosotros / vosotras)	we add -ÍS	Vosotros / vosotras partís
second-person plural (ustedes)	we add -EN	Ustedes parten
third-person singular (él / ella)	we add -E	Él / ella parte
third-person plural (ellos / ellas)	we add -EN	Ellos / ellas parten

Vocabulary: fruits, vegetables, food

Here's a vocabulary list of the food mentioned in this chapter.

- *los mariscos* means "shellfish"
- *la empanada* is like a turnover with savory filling
- *el pulpo* means "octopus"
- *el guisado* means "stew"
- *el pastel* means "cake"
- *el tomate* means "tomato"
- *el atún* means "tuna"
- *el pollo* means "chicken"
- *la lechuga* means "lettuce"
- *el pan* means "bread"
- *la manzana* means "apple"
- *el arroz* means "rice"
- *el jamón* means "ham"
- *los lácteos* means "dairy products"
- *el queso* means "cheese"
- *la leche* means "milk"
- *la nata* means "cream"
- *el yogur* means "yogurt"
- *los fiambres* means "cold cuts"
- *la fruta* means "fruit"

- *la verdura* means "vegetables"
- *la zanahoria* means "carrot"
- *el pepino* means "cucumber"
- *la patata* means "potato"
- *la calabaza* means "pumpkin"
- *la piña* means "pineapple"
- *la naranja* means "orange"
- *la fresa* means "strawberry"
- *la ciruela* means "plum"
- *el huevo* means "egg"
- *el aceite* means "oil"
- *la galleta* means "cookie"

Culture Section: Traditional Spanish Meals

We've already mentioned a few traditional Spanish meals, but since I wanted to learn how to cook a local dish, Julio and I went online to find a recipe that wouldn't be so hard. Finally, I decided I wanted to make *una tortilla de patatas* (an omelet made with onions, fried potatoes, and eggs), but here's some of the information I gathered during my research.

La paella valenciana is a rice dish cooked in a circular pan that's also called *paella*. Besides the rice, the dish has onions, peppers, mussels, chicken, shrimp, and tomatoes. As you can tell from its name, it's originally from Valencia (an eastern autonomous community), but nowadays is prepared all over Spain.

El cocido madrileño is a hearty stew consisting of three parts: broth, chickpeas and vegetables, and meats (chicken, pork, and cold cuts). Originally, it was a dish prepared by farmers to endure cold days working in the field. That's why it's so caloric, ideal for winter.

El gazpacho andaluz is a soup served cold, which makes sense since it's originally from the warm south of Spain. The soup (or juice?) is made of tomatoes, onion, garlic, and cucumber, and it's usually served with fresh bread and olive oil.

Last but not least, we have *la crema catalana*. This world-famous dessert is quite easy to make. First, you must cook the ingredients (egg yolk, milk, sugar, flour, lemon and cinnamon) together to obtain the custard. Then, you have to sprinkle lots of sugar on top of it and burn it to make a thin and hard layer.

Exercises

1. True or false: To decide which demonstrative pronoun to use, you only need to consider the gender and number of the noun it's replacing.

2. Which are the three distances that determine which demonstrative pronoun to use?

3. If you wanted to point to a singular, feminine noun like *roca,* which is far from you but close to the person you are talking to, which of these demonstrative pronouns would you use?
   a. Estas   b. Esa   c. Aquel

4. If you wanted to point to a group of masculine nouns like *carros* which are far from you and from the person you are talking to, which of these demonstrative pronouns would you use?
   a. Esos   b. Estas   c. Aquello

5. Do you remember one of the ways to ask for the price of something?

6. If you asked for a price, which of these answers can you expect to hear?
   a. Precia
   b. Vale
   c. Los precious son

7. True or false: *quién* is the singular equivalent of English "who."

8. Which of the following interrogative pronouns are used in the same way as English "which"?
   a. Cuánto/cuánta
      b. Cuando
   c. Cuál/cuáles

9. Complete with the correct interrogative pronoun:
   ¿(Who).... vienen a la fiesta?

10. True or false: *poco* means "too much."

11. Cross the odd one out:
    a. Mucho   b. Demasiado   c. Nada   d. Más
    e. Muy

12. For the present simple of the first-person plural
    (*nosotros/nosotras*), the conjugation of the verb *temer* is
    tememos. Which is the correct conjugation of *correr*?
    a. Corremos   b. Corro   c. Corren   d. Corremas

13. Complete with the correct form of the regular verbs of the
    first conjugation:
    (amar) Yo amo.
    (cantar) Yo cant...
    (bailar) Yo ...

14. Complete with the correct form of the regular verbs of the
    second conjugation:

    (temer) Tú temes.
    (beber) Tú beb...
    (comer) Tú ...

15. Complete with the correct form of the regular verbs of the
    third conjugation:
    (partir) Ella parte.
    (salir) Ella sal...
    (vivir) Ella ...

16. True or false: *zanahoria* means "cucumber."

17. What's the Spanish word for "pumpkin"?
    a. Patata   b. Calabaza   c. Naranja

18. Choose the odd one out:
    a. Atún   b. Pollo   c. Pastel   d.
    Pulpo

19. True or false: Cheese, milk and cream are *lácteos.*

20. Choose the odd one out:
    a. Naranja   b. Piña   c. Ciruela   d. Aceite
    d. Fresa

Chapter 5: Going Sightseeing

Hi! It's Sarah here. After visiting Galicia, we traveled southeast from Santiago de Compostela to Salamanca. It was a short 4-hour journey, but it gave us the time to practice some Spanish and for Julio to tell me about the history of Salamanca. We arrived at around 11 a.m.

Do you remember that Julio told us that Castile is where the Castilian language first started? Well, Salamanca is one of the nine provinces that form the autonomous community of Castile and León. Here, they not only speak Spanish and Castilian but also Leonese and Galician, two varieties that are protected due to their cultural value.

Castile and Leon borders Portugal and is home to eight UNESCO World Heritage Sites – of which I visited the only one in Salamanca, the historical center or "Old City of Salamanca." Salamanca is famous for its history, its monuments, and its food. Its University is one of the oldest in the whole of Europe and has some very imposing buildings.

Julio has some friends here, so we visited them, and I put my new Spanish knowledge to the test, but he stayed with them during the afternoon, and I wanted to go sightseeing a bit on my own. It was a challenge because I could no longer have Julio translate things for me and encourage me to speak in Spanish – but we were already in the middle of our trip, so I had to start getting more confident, right?

We visited María and Rubén, Julio's friends, and after our introductions, which I'm almost an expert at already, I asked them for a few directions so that I could start my solo journey.

Luckily, their house is near the city center; they live on the corner of calle Zamora and Calle de las Isabeles. I wanted to start my journey on Plaza Mayor, the most iconic place in Salamanca. It was built in the 18th century, its design is typically baroque, and it has many bars, cafés, and restaurants where I wanted to eat a typical *hornazo*, a kind of meat pie stuffed with pork loin, chorizo, and eggs. It is a typical dish from Salamanca and Ávila only, so it was my opportunity to try it for lunch. I asked María and Rubén how to get from their house to plaza Mayor and then to la Casa de las Conchas, a historical building that is now a public library.

This is how our conversation went:

● ¿Cómo llego a plaza Mayor desde aquí?	● How do I get to plaza Mayor from here?
○ Bueno, simplemente tienes que continuar derecho por calle Zamora hasta que termina la calle. Allí está la plaza Mayor. Para entrar, tienes que doblar a la izquierda e ir hasta la esquina de plaza Mayor y calle Toro. Luego doblas a la derecha. A mitad de cuadra encontrarás una entrada a la plaza.	○ Well, you just need to continue straight through Zamora street until the end of the street. There is plaza Mayor. To go in, you have to turn left and go to the corner of plaza Mayor and calle Toro. Then you turn right. In the middle of the block, you'll find an entrance to the square.
● Perfecto. Gracias. ¿Dónde me recomienda comer hornazo allí?	● Awesome. Thank you. Where would you recommend to eat hornazo there?

○ Te recomendamos la confitería Santa Lucía. Puedes encontrarla al lado de la entrada a plaza Mayor.	○ We recommend Santa Lucía coffee shop. You can find it next to the entrance to plaza Mayor.
● ¡Gracias! ¿Y cómo voy de allí a la Casa de las Conchas?	● Thank you! And how do I go from there to Casa de Conchas?
○ Después de la confitería Santa Lucía, puedes salir de la plaza por la Plaza del Poeta Iglesias hasta llegar a la calle Quintana. Allí doblas a la derecha y luego a la izquierda en la primera calle. Esa es la ruta Mayor. Debes caminar por allí hasta la diagonal Rúa Antigua y encontrarás la Casa de las Conchas.	○ After Sants Lucía coffee shop, you can exit the square through Plaza del Poeta Iglesias until reaching Quintana street. There, you turn right, and then left on the first street. That is Mayor road. You have to walk that way until reaching Rúa Antigua diagonal. There you'll find Casa de las Conchas.
● Perfecto. ¡Gracias!	● Awesome. Thanks!

I ended up visiting plaza Mayor and its surroundings; I ate *hornazo* and had *tocinillo de cielo* for dessert, similar to a *flan* or pudding. Then, I went to Casa de las Conchas and La Clerecía, the building right across the street. Nowadays, it belongs to the Pontifical University of Salamanca, but it was built in the 17th century. I could actually go up one of its towers and see the whole city center. After that, I used my new phrases to ask about the way to the New and Old Cathedrals, so I walked a short distance and went there as well.

To ask for directions, I had a short interaction with someone walking nearby:

• Disculpe, ¿dónde está la catedral? ¿Está cerca?	• Excuse me, where's the cathedral? Is it close?
○ Sí, está a unos 200 metros.	○ Yes, it's about 200 metres away.
• ¿Podría decirme cómo llegar?	• Could you tell me how to get there?
○ Claro. Ve todo derecho por la ruta Mayor y lo encontrarás a tu izquierda. Son unas dos cuadras.	○ Of course. Go straight through Mayor road and you'll see it to your left. It's about two blocks away.
• ¡Muchas gracias!	• Thank you very much!

I admit that I was pretty nervous when I had to talk in Spanish for the first time without Julio to back me up, but now I feel much more confident!

As for my trip, I also wanted to visit some of Salamanca's museums, but I had run out of time for the day. So I went back to María and Rubén's house, and we went to a restaurant for dinner. Then, we stayed the night at their place.

Now, Julio will teach you a bit of vocabulary, grammar, and all the useful phrases so that you can travel on your own too.

Transportation

Hi! It's Julio here again. While Sarah traveled around Salamanca and visited some of its landmarks, I stayed with Rubén and María. But, of course, she didn't leave without a few lessons first.

Okay, so for a bit of vocabulary, here is the Spanish name of a few means of transportation that might come in handy for your trip:

- *El tren* means "train"
- *El autobús* means "bus"
- *El avión* means "airplane"
- *El taxi* means "taxi"
- *La bicicleta* means "bike"

- *El automóvil* means "car"
- *La motocicleta* means "motorcycle"
- *El metro* means "subway"
- *El barco* means "ship"

So as an example, we can say the following sentence: "Viajamos de Atlanta a Barcelona en avión y de Barcelona a Bilbao en tren." And let's add: "Hoy viajamos de Santiago de Compostela a Salamanca en tren."

And, you can always go places *a pie*, which means "on foot"!

Buildings

When you're in a different city, everything might look different, but the names of the buildings stay the same, right? Well, here's a list of some buildings that can be found in almost any city:

- *La casa* means "house"
- *El apartamento* means "apartment
- *El museo* means "museum"
- *La plaza* means "square"
- *La catedral* means "cathedral"
- *La iglesia* means "church"
- *La biblioteca* means "library"
- *El cine* means "cinema"
- *El supermercado* means "supermarket"
- *El hospital* means "hospital"
- *El banco* means "bank"
- *El restaurante* means "restaurant"
- *El aeropuerto* means "airport"
- *La estación de tren* means "train station"
- *Universidad* means "university"
- *Farmacia* means "pharmacy"

For example, the buildings that Sarah visited today are: *la plaza, la biblioteca, y la catedral.*

Asking for directions

Asking for directions can be difficult in a new language, but here's a list of phrases that will definitely help you get where you want to!

- *Disculpe* means "Excuse me." It is used to get someone's attention, and it's pronounced /dees - kool - peh/.

- *Perdone* also means "excuse me."

- *¿Dónde está...?* means "Where is...?" It should be followed by the name of the place you want to get to.

- *¿Cómo llego a...?* means "How do I get to...?" This one should also be followed by the name of the place.

- *¿Cómo voy a...?* also means "How do it get to...?" and should also be followed by the name of the place.

- *¿Podría decirme cómo llegar a...?* means "Could you tell me how to get to...?" This one should also be followed by the name of the place.

- *¿... está cerca?* means "Is ... nearby?" This one should be preceded by the name of the place you want to get to.

- *¿Sabe si hay algún/alguna... por aquí?* means "do you know if there is a ... nearby?" The ellipsis should be filled with the name of the place you want to go to, and the decision between *algún* or *alguna* depends on the gender of the following word.

- *¿... está en esta calle?* means "Is... on this street?" It should be preceded by the name of the place you want to get to.

Adverbs of Place

Now, of course, you need to understand the directions people will give you in Spanish. So here are the most common adverbs of place in Spanish that you might hear when someone is giving direction, and you can also add them to your questions.

- *Aquí* means "here"
- *Allí* means "there"
- *Dentro de* means "inside"
- *Afuera de* means "outside"

- *Adelante* means "ahead"
- *Detrás* means "behind"
- *Abajo* means "below"
- *Arriba* means "above"
- *A la derecha* means "to/on the right"
- *A la izquierda* means "to/on the left"
- *Al lado de* means "besides" or "next to"
- *En frente de* means "in front of"
- *Al final de* means "at the end"
- *Alrededor* means "around"
- *En el medio* means "in the middle"
- *Cerca* means "near"
- *Lejos* means "far"
- *Entre* means "between"
- *En la esquina* means "on the corner"

Giving Directions

Okay, now it's time to learn some possible answers when you ask for directions – and to learn to give them yourself!

The first thing you need to know is that we can use the verb *estar* to say where something is using some other place as a reference. For example, we can say *La confitería Santa Lucía* **está** *al lado de la entrada de la plaza Mayor* ("The coffee shop Santa Lucía is beside the entrance to plaza Mayor") *or La catedral está en frente del restaurante* ("The cathedral is in front of the restaurant"), and you can also say *La Casa de las Conchas está al final de la calle* ("La Casa de las Conchas is at the end of the street"). You can use *estar* with all of the adverbs from the previous section!

- *Tienes que seguir derecho/recto* means "you have to go straight on"
- *Dobla a la izquierda/derecha* means "turn left/right"
- *Gira a la derecha/izquierda* means "turn right/left"
- *Cruza la calle* means "cross the street"
- *Continúa por esta calle* means "continue on this street"

- *Está a ... calles* means "It's... blocks away." The ellipsis should be filled with the number of blocks.

Asking for Tickets

Once you get to the place you want to go to, you should be able to ask for tickets. Otherwise, how will you get in? These are a few phrases that might come in handy when you are doing an activity:

- *Una entrada para..., por favor* means "A ticket for..., please." The gap should be filled with the name of a movie or play, or even the name of a museum or other type of activity. For example, *una entrada para el museo, por favor* ("one ticket for the museum, please"). If you want more than one ticket, you simply need to change the number and remember to make *entrada* a plural.

- *¿Me podría dar una entrada para...?* means "Could you give me a ticket for...?" In Spanish, we sometimes use this polite structure and don't say "please," because we consider it polite enough. However, you can add a *por favor* at the end of the question if you prefer it. Again, the gap should be filled with the name of a movie, play, museum, etc.

- *¿Tiene un mapa de...?* means "Do you have a map of the...?" Whether a map of the city center, the whole country, or a museum, you simply need to fill the gap with the place you need a map of.

- *¿A qué hora cierran?* means "When do you close?"

Present Form of Some Irregular Verbs

Well, it's time to go back to grammar now. In the previous chapter, we've seen the conjugation of some regular verbs, but now it's time to see the conjugation of some irregular ones besides *ser* and *estar*.

In this table, you will find the present form of some irregular verbs

	HACER	IR	HABER	TRAER	TENER
yo	hago	voy	he	traigo	tengo
tú	haces	vas	has	traes	tienes
él / ella	hace	va	ha	trae	tiene
nosotros / nosotras	hacemos	vamos	hemos	traemos	tenemos
vosotros / vosotras	hacéis	vais	habéis	traéis	tenéis
ellos / ellas / ustedes	hacen	van	han	traen	tienen

As you see, the ending of these conjugations is not always different from the ending of regular verbs, but generally what changes is the root of the verb.

Present Progressive Tense

In Spanish, the present progressive tense is conveyed through a verbal phrase that uses the conjugation of *estar* + a gerund (a "gerund" is the noun form of a verb that ends in -ing). One example of this could be *Estoy comiendo*, which means "I'm eating."

We've already seen the conjugation of *estar*, and we almost know it by heart, right? So let's talk about the gerunds.

In Spanish, gerunds are not conjugated depending on the person. Good news, right? They remain unchanged and are used for talking about things happening – that is, for the progressive tense!

The gerund is formed in the following way:

- Infinitive verbs ending in *-ar* end in *-ando* in the gerund. For example: *cantar* turns into *cantando*.

- Infinitive verbs ending in *-ir* or *-er* end in *-iendo* in the gerund. For example, *comer* and *salir* turn into *comiendo* and *saliendo*.

As we've said, the gerund is never conjugated, but to form the progressive, the verb *estar* does need to be conjugated. For this reason, we could say *él está comiendo* and *vosotras estáis comiendo*.

Time Markers for the Present

Some time markers usually trigger the present in different sentences. For example, we would usually use the present with words like "always" in English.

As we've seen, we use the present to talk about things that are generally true, so these are a few phrases that might signal that a present form follows:

- Todos los días ("Every day")
- Los lunes ("Every Monday"). Of course, you could use any other day of the week.
- Siempre ("Always")
- En general ("Generally")
- Usualmente ("Usually")
- Casi nunca ("Hardly ever")
- Nunca ("Never")

On the other hand, there are also time markers that trigger the present progressive tense, like:

- *Ahora* ("Now")
- *Ahora mismo* ("Right now")
- *En este momento* ("At this moment")

Verb Moods

Unlike English, Spanish can have several verb moods. So far, we've only seen the indicative or *indicativo* used for real situations. But there are two more moods: the subjunctive and imperative.

The imperative mood is used to give commands or strong requests. In Spanish, the imperative is also a tense with its own conjugations. One example could be: *Come todo lo que tienes en el plato* ("Eat everything on your plate"). On the other hand, the subjunctive mood is used to express wishes, suggestions, desires, or to   talk about hypotheses. In Spanish, there are three tenses with their own conjugations in the subjunctive mood: *presente de subjuntivo, futuro de subjuntivo* y *pretérito imperfecto de subjuntivo.* An example of the *presente de subjuntivo* could be *Es increíble que coma todo* ("It is amazing how he eats everything"); an example of the *futuro de subjuntivo* could be *Aunque él comiere todo mañana, no le daré un premio* ("Even if he eats everything tomorrow, I won't give him a reward"); and lastly, an example of the *pretérito imperfecto de subjuntivo* could be *Me dijo que comiera todo* ("She told me that I should eat everything").

Exercises

1. How do you say "bike" in Spanish?
2. What does *autobús* mean in English?
3. How do you say "museum" in Spanish? And what about "square"?
4. What do *iglesia* and *estación de tren* mean?
5. What would you say first when you come up to someone to ask for directions?
6. How would you ask how to get to the library?
7. How would you ask whether there is a pharmacy nearby?
8. If the university is next to the library, it is...
    a. en frente
    b. b. arriba
    c. al lado
9. If there is a statue in the middle of a square, it is...
    a. en el medio
    b. afuera
    c. en la esquina

10. If someone told you *Cruza la calle y dobla a la izquierda*, what would you do?

    a. continue on this street and turn right.

    b. cross the street and turn left

    c. go straight on.

11. If you had to give directions, how would you say "turn right and walk straight on for 3 blocks"?

12. How would you ask for three tickets to the museum?

13. What is the second person singular present form of the verb *traer*?

    a. traemos

    b. traigo

    c. traes

14. What is the first person plural present form of the verb *haber*?

    a. he

    b. hemos

    c. han

15. True or false: The Spanish present progressive tense is formed with the conjugated form of the verb *estar* and a gerund.

16. True or false: if there is a verb that ends in *-ir* or *-er* in the infinitive form, the gerund form ends in *-ando*.

17. How would you say "I am singing" in Spanish?

18. Which of the following is **not** a time marker for the present progressive?

    a. todos los días

    b. ahora mismo

    c. en este momento

19. Which of the following is **not** a time marker for the present progressive?

    a. siempre

    b. casi nunca

    c. ahora

20. True or false: the subjunctive mode is used for real situations.

Quiz

We're already halfway through our journey, so it's time to take a little quiz to review everything we've seen so far.

Unlike in the *exercises*, each right answer will be worth a point in this quiz. If you get 15-20 right answers, you're definitely great at this; keep it up! If you get 10-15 points, you're doing great, and I hope this quiz has helped with your doubts. But if your score is below 10, I encourage you to go back to the first five chapters to revise the information before moving on.

1. Regarding accents, what kind of word is *gorrión*? How would you pronounce the G and the double R?

2. Is this sentence grammatically correct? *Lucía juega al fútbol, son muy buenos.*

3. How do you ask someone how old they are in Spanish? And how do you answer?

4. Can you name the Spanish indefinite articles? When do you use each of them?

5. How would you ask if you can pay in cash?

6. How do you form yes/no questions in Spanish?

7. Which preposition would you use to say "I walk towards the museum"?

8. Which of these objects does not belong in the bathroom?

    a. *toalla*

    b. *pasta de diente*

    c. *cama*

    d. *jabón*

    e. *peine*

9. Which characteristics of the noun do you need to consider in choosing the correct demonstrative pronoun?

10. At a store, how would you ask how much is the chicken? How would the store clerk answer that it costs 20€?

11. What does *cuánto* mean? What is the difference between *cuánto* and *cuántos*?

12. How would you ask "Why are the pumpkins so expensive"?

13. At a store, how would you ask "Where are the cakes?"

14. Using adverbs of quantity, how would you say "It's too much for a few days"?

15. Can you conjugate the verb *amar* in the present with the pronouns *yo, tú, ella, nosotras, vosotras,* and *ellas*?

16. Can you conjugate the verb *temer* in the present with the pronouns *yo, tú, él, nosotros, vosotros,* and *ellos*?

17. Can you conjugate the verb *partir* in the present with the pronouns *yo, tú, ella, nosotras, vosotras,* and *ellas*?

18. How would you ask "How do I get to the supermarket?" in Spanish? And how would you answer that question if you had to turn right, walk straight on for 3 blocks and then turn left?

19. Can you conjugate the verbs *ser* and *estar* in the present with the pronouns *yo, tú, él, nosotros, vosotros,* and *ellos*?

20. What is the difference between these two sentences: *Paula come pizza y toma vino* and *Paula está comiendo pizza y tomando vino*?

Despite how you did in this quiz, keep up the good work! We're halfway there, and this journey still has a lot in store for you!

Chapter 6: Having a House Party

After our lovely days in Salamanca, we took a bus to Seville, the sunniest city in Spain and the capital of the autonomous community of Andalusia. Located in the southwest of the Iberian Peninsula, the city is crossed by the River Guadalquivir. It's known for the Moorish castles, the medieval streets, the smell of orange blossoms, and the celebration of *Semana Santa* (Holy Week), one of the city's most important festivities.

Talking About your Family

During the six-hour bus ride, Julio was very excited because a big part of his family lives in Seville. So, during the journey, he started talking about all of them. At first, I was a bit confused because I didn't know the words to talk about family members.

● Mi madrina nos va a estar esperando en la estación de autobús.	● My godmother will be waiting for us at the bus station.
○ ¿Tu madre?	○ Your mother?
● No, mi madrina es la hermana de mi madre.	● No, my godmother is my mother's sister.

○ Ah, madrina es "aunt."	○ Ah, godmother is "tía."
● No, "aunt" es tía. Lo que pasa es que Carola, ese es su nombre, es mi tía y mi madrina.	● No, "tía" is an aunt. The thing is that Carola, that's her name, is my aunt and my godmother.
○ Bien, creo que entiendo. Entonces su esposo es tu padrino.	○ Okay, I think I understand. Then her husband is your godfather.
● No, su esposo, José, es mi tío, pero no es mi padrino. Mi padrino es Luis, un cuñado de mi padre.	● No, her husband, Jose, is my uncle, but he's not my godfather. My godfather is Luis, my father's brother-in-law.
○ ¿Cuñado? ¿Qué significa eso?	○ ¿Brother-in-law? What does that mean?
● Significa que está casado con su hermana, mi tía Cecilia. Ellos son los padres de Pancho y Josefa, mis primos.	● It means he's married to his sister, my aunt Cecilia. They are the parents of Pancho and Josefa, my cousins.
○ Ay, Julio, un poco más despacio, que me pierdo con tantas palabras nuevas.	○ Oh, Julio, a bit slower, I get lost with so many new words.
● No te preocupes que vas a conocerlos a todos el sábado, en la cena que organizó mi abuela Teresa.	● Don't worry, you'll meet them all on Saturday at my grandmother Teresa's dinner.

As I was going to meet his family in Seville, he took the time to explain to me his family tree, and he taught me all the words to talk about family members.

Family Members

Julio started with the words for the closest relatives:

- *La abuela* is "the grandmother"
- *El abuelo* is "the grandfather"

- *Los abuelos* are "the grandparents"
- *La madre* is "the mother"
- *El padre* is "the father"
- *Los padres* are "the parents"
- *La tía* is "the aunt"
- *El tío* is "the uncle"
- *La hermana* is "the sister"
- *El hermano* is "the brother"
- *La prima* is "the female cousin"
- *El primo* is "the male cousin"
- *La hija* is "the daughter"
- *El hijo* is "the son"
- *La nieta* is "the granddaughter"
- *El nieto* is "the grandson"
- *La sobrina* is "the niece"
- *El sobrino* is "the nephew"
- *La esposa* is "the wife"
- *El esposo* or *el marido* is "the husband"

Then, he moved on to the stepfamily:

- *La madrastra* is "the stepmother"
- *El padrastro* is "the stepfather"
- *La hermanastra* is "the stepsister," the daughter of your parent's spouse
- *El hermanastro* is "the stepbrother," the son of your parent's spouse
- *La media hermana* is "the half-sister," a female sibling by one parent
- *El medio hermano* is "the half-brother," a male sibling by one parent
- *La hijastra* is the "stepdaughter"
- *El hijastro* is "the stepson"

Finally, he delved into the extended family:

- *La madrina* is "the godmother"
- *El padrino* is "the godfather"
- *La ahijada* is "the goddaughter"
- *El ahijado* is "the godson"
- *La suegra* is "the mother-in-law"
- *El suegro* is "the father-in-law"
- *La cuñada* is "the sister-in-law"
- *El cuñado* is "the brother-in-law"
- *La nuera* is "the daughter-in-law"
- *El yerno* is "the son-in-law"

Describing People

When we arrived, Julio's aunt and godmother, Carola, picked us up and took us around the city. She showed us the Cathedral (the third-largest church in Europe), the Plaza de España, the Torre de Oro (a watchtower in the River Guadalquivir), and Seville's Old City district.

I was a bit nervous about the dinner party that Teresa, Julio's grandmother, had organized for Saturday. I was afraid I would mix up all of Julio's relatives. To make it easier for me, Julio made me a list of everyone who was going, and he added a short description of them:

Mi abuela Teresa es baja y delgada. Tiene el pelo corto y blanco. Su tez es clara. Tiene los ojos redondos y marrones.	My grandmother Teresa is short and thin. She's got short, white hair. Her complexion is pale. Her eyes are round and brown.
Mi tío José, el marido de Carola, es alto y fornido. Tiene la cara alargada, con una nariz aguileña. Sus ojos son oscuros, y su pelo es negro y ondulado.	My uncle Jose, Carola's husband, is tall and stout. His face is elongated, with an aquiline nose. His eyes are dark, and his hair is black and wavy.

Mi tía Cecilia tiene el pelo rubio, largo y lacio, aunque siempre lo lleva recogido en un rodete. Es esbelta y viste elegante. Sus ojos son claros. Está casada con Luis, mi padrino.	My aunt Cecilia has long, straight blond hair, although she always has it tucked in a bun. She's slim and she dresses elegantly. Her eyes are clear. She's married to Luis, my godfather.
Luis es alto y desgarbado. Su cara es cuadrada y de tez oscura. Sus ojos también son oscuros. Su pelo es negro y encrespado, y siempre lo lleva corto.	Luis is tall and ungainly. He has a square face and dark skin. His eyes are also dark. His hair is black and frizzy, and he always wears it short.
Mi prima Josefa es joven, tiene 20 años. Es flaca y baja de estatura. Tiene ojos celestes y un aro en la nariz. Siempre lleva el pelo teñido de colores brillantes. No sé de qué color lo tendrá ahora, pero la vas a reconocer.	My cousin Josefa is young, she's 20 years old. She's skinny and short. She's got blue eyes and a nose ring. She always dyes her hair bright colors. I don't know which color it is now, but you'll recognize her.
Mi primo Pancho es pecoso y tiene el pelo pelirrojo. Es grande y musculoso, le gusta mucho hacer deporte.	My cousin Pancho has freckles and red hair. He is big and muscular, he really likes sports.

Adjectives for Describing Appearances

- *Tipo de cuerpo* means "body shape"
  - *Alto/a* means "tall"
  - *Bajo/a* means "short"
  - *Corpulento/a* means "stout"
  - *Delgado/a* means "lean"
  - *Desgarbado/a* means "lanky"
  - *Esbelto/a* means "slender"

- *Flaco/a* means "skinny"
- *Grande* means "large"
- *Menudo/a* means "petite"
- *Musculoso/a* means "muscular"
- *La cara is* "the face"
  - *Barbudo/a* means "bearded"
  - *Cuadrado/a* means "square"
  - *Largo/a* means "long"
  - *Ovalado/a* means "oval"
  - *Pecoso/a* means "freckled"
  - *Redondo/a* means "round"
- *Los ojos* are "the eyes"
  - *Abierto/a* means "open"
  - *Azul* means "blue"
  - *Claro/a* means "light-colored"
  - *Marrón* means "brown"
  - *Negro/a* means "black"
  - *Oscuro/a* means "dark"
  - *Redondo/a* means "round"
  - *Verde* means "green"
- *El pelo* or *el cabello* is "the hair"
  - *Abundante* means "thick"
  - *Brillante* means "shiny"
  - *Calvo/a* means "bald
  - *Canoso/a* means "grey"
  - *Castaño/a* means "brown"
  - *Corto/a* means "short"
  - *Encrespado/a* means "frizzy"
  - *Fino/a* means "thin"
  - *Lacio/a* means "straight"
  - *Largo/a* means "long"

- *Negro/a* means "black"
- *Ondulado/a* means "wavy"
- *Pelirrojo/a* means "red"
- *Rizado/a* means "curly"
- *Rubio/a* means "blonde"
- *Teñido/a* means "dyed"
- *La nariz* is "the nose"
  - *Aguileño/a* means "hooked"
  - *Ancho/a* means "wide"
  - *Angosto/a* means "narrow"
  - *Recto/a* means "straight"
  - *Respingado/a* means "turned-up"
  - *Torcido/a* means "crooked"
- *La edad* is "the age"
  - *Viejo/a* means "old"
  - *Joven* means "young"
  - *Arrugado/a* means "wrinkly"
  - *De mediana edad* means "middle-aged"
  - *Juvenil* means "youthful"
  - *Entrado/a en años* means "elderly"

Gender of Adjectives

When I gave Sarah this list of adjectives to describe people's appearance, she noticed that many had two endings, so I explained the gender of adjectives.

Adjectives are used to describe nouns, so they have to agree in gender (and number) with the noun they describe. Many nouns that end in -A are feminine, and many nouns that end in -O are masculine, and the same happens with the adjectives. For example, I said *Mi abuela Teresa es baja*, but if I was referring to a man, I would have said *Su hermano es bajo*.

Maybe you've noticed that, on the list, some adjectives have only one ending. These adjectives are invariable: they don't change depending on the gender of the noun they describe. For example, we say *Su cabello* (masculine noun) *es oscuro y abundante*, but *Su cabellera* (feminine noun) *es oscura y abundante*. As you can see, the adjective *abundante* stays invariable, while *oscura/oscuro* change depending on the gender of the noun.

Adjectives also vary depending on the number of the noun. To make an adjective plural, you just need to add -S or -ES at the end. For example: *Sus ojos son claros*.

And finally, don't forget that adjectives normally go after the noun in Spanish.

The Human Body

To describe my family, I mentioned some parts of the body. Here we have some more:

- *El cuerpo* is "the body"
- *Los labios* are "the lips"
- *La espalda* is "the back"
- *El pie* is "the foot"
- *El dedo* is "the finger"
- *El dedo del pie* is "the toe"
- *La cabeza* is "the head"
- *El cuello* is "the neck"
- *La mano* is "the hand"
- *La pierna* is "the leg"
- *El tobillo* is "the ankle"
- *La boca* is "the mouth"
- *El diente* is "the tooth"
- *La uña* is "the nail"
- *El hombro* is the "the shoulder"
- *El brazo* is "the arm"
- *El estómago* is the "the stomach"
- *La rodilla* is "the knee"
- *El codo* is "the elbow"
- *La oreja* is "the ear"

Possessive Adjectives and Pronouns

Possessive adjectives and pronouns are the words we use to show that something belongs to someone. Possessive adjectives go together with the noun, for example: *Esa es **mi** casa* ("That's my house"). Possessive pronouns replace the noun, for example: *La **mía** no se ve desde aquí* ("Mine is not visible from here"). Note that in Spanish, possessive pronouns and adjectives agree with what they describe (not with the person who owns the thing). And, as you can see, possessive pronouns go together with a definite article (*la*, in the example), which also needs to agree with the gender of the thing owned.

- Possessive adjectives

	Singular		Plural	
	Masculine	*Feminine*	*Masculine*	*Feminine*
"My" (belonging to me)	*Mi*	*Mi*	*Mis*	*Mis*
"Your" (belonging to someone you address as *tú*)	*Tu*	*Tu*	*Tus*	*Tus*
"His," "her," "its," "your" (belonging to someone you address as *usted*)	*Su*	*Su*	*Sus*	*Sus*
"Our" (belonging to us)	*Nuestro*	*Nuestra*	*Nuestros*	*Nuestras*

"Your" (belonging to people you address as *vosotros/ vosotras*)	*Vuestro*	*Vuestra*	*Vuestros*	*Vuestras*
"Their," "your" (belonging to people you address as *ustedes*)	*Su*	*Su*	*Sus*	*Sus*

- Possessive pronouns (together with the article)

	Singular		Plural	
	Masculine	*Feminine*	*Masculine*	*Feminine*
"Mine" (belonging to me)	*El mío*	*La mía*	*Los míos*	*Las mías*
"Yours" (belonging to someone you address as *tú*)	*El tuyo*	*La tuya*	*Los tuyos*	*Las tuyas*
"His," "hers," "its," "yours" (belonging to someone you address as *usted*)	*El suyo*	*La suya*	*Los suyos*	*Las suyas*

"Ours" (belonging to us)	El nuestro	La nuestra	Los nuestros	Las nuestras
"Yours" (belonging to people you address as *vosotros/ vosotras*)	El vuestro	La vuestra	Los vuestros	Las vuestras
"Theirs," "yours" (belonging to people you address as *ustedes*)	El suyo	La suya	Los suyos	Las suyas

Some examples:

- **-Mi** padre vive en Barcelona, ¿**el tuyo**? -**El mío** vive en Washington DC.
- **Sus** hermanas son mellizas.
- ¿**Tus** padres están divorciados? **Los suyos** están casados.
- **-Nuestras** familias no se conocen. ¿**Las vuestras**? -**Las nuestras** se conocieron el año pasado.

Objective Pronouns

- Direct Object

The direct object (DO) is the person or thing that receives the action of the verb. Both in Spanish and in English, we can replace the DO with a pronoun once we've already mentioned it, for example: ***Su pelo** es largo, aunque siempre **lo** lleva recogido* ("She has long hair, but she always wears it up"). As you can see in the example, **lo** is replacing ***su pelo***. Have you noticed the change in the word order? When we replace the DO for a pronoun, we put it before the verb. Also, note that the objective pronoun has to agree in gender and number with the noun that's being replaced. Take a look at this list of all the different direct object pronouns.

	Masculine	Feminine
"Me" (first person singular)	*Me*	*Me*
"You" (second person singular *tú*)	*Te*	*Te*
"Him," "her," "it" (third person singular); "you" (second person singular *usted*)	*Lo*	*La*
"Us" (first person plural)	*Nos*	*Nos*
"You" (second person plural *vosotros/vosotras*)	*Os*	*Os*
"Them" (third person plural); "you" (second person plural *ustedes*)	*Los*	*Las*

Some examples:

- Mi madre adoptó un perro. **Lo** encontró abandonado en la calle ("My mother adopted a dog. She found it abandoned on the street").

- La abuela de Julio **me** invitó a la cena ("Julio's grandmother invited me for dinner").

- Compré unas flores y se **las** llevé de regalo ("I bought flowers and gave them to her as a present").

- Indirect Object

The indirect object (IO) is the person or thing the action is intended to benefit or harm. To distinguish it from the DO, you can ask yourself to whom the direct object is given to. Take a look at this example: *La abuela le compró a Julio un regalo* ("His grandmother bought Julio a present"), where *a present* is the DO, and *a Julio*, to whom the DO is given to, is the IO.

The IO sometimes is duplicated, like in the example above: *le* (an indirect object pronoun) also means *a Julio*. When the person or thing that receives the DO is understood from context, you can leave out the construction *a* + noun and have only the pronoun, for example. *Como era el cumpleaños de Julio, la abuela le compró un regalo.* Take a look at the list of the indirect object pronouns:

"Me," "to me," "for me" (first person singular)	*Me*
"You," "to you," "for you" (second person singular *tú*)	*Te*
"Him/Her/It," "to him/her/it," "for him/her/it" (third person singular); "You," "to you," "for you" (second person singular *usted*)	*Le*
"Us," "for us," "to us" (first person plural)	*Nos*
"You," "to you," "for you" (second person plural *vosotros/vosotras*)	*Os*
"Them," to them," "for them" (third person plural); "you," "to you," "for you" (second person plural *ustedes*)	*Les*

Some examples:

- La abuela de Julio nos invitó a cenar, y nosotros **le** respondimos la invitación ("Julio's grandmother invited us for dinner, and we answered the invitation").

- La abuela de Julio **me** agradeció el regalo ("Julio's grandmother thanked me for the present").

- Luego de comer, todos **le** ofrecimos ayuda para levantar la mesa ("After dinner, we all offered her our help clearing the table").

The last thing we did before the dinner party was buy a gift for the hostess. In Spain, it's common to get invited to dine at someone's house, even if you don't know them very well. A gift is not expected, but I didn't want to arrive empty-handed. Julio said that his grandmother probably had already thought of the wine and dessert that matched the dinner, so I settled for a nice flower bouquet. In the end, the dinner party was a total success.

Exercises

1. True or false: *Abuela* means grandfather.
2. Cross the odd one out.
   a. Hermanastra   b. Prima   c. Media hermana
        d. Tío
3. True or false: *Marido* and *esposo* both mean "husband."
4. What is the Spanish word to talk about your children's female partner?
5. What is the Spanish word to talk about your partner's father?
6. True or false: *Esbelto/a, bajo/a* and *rizado/a* are used to describe the body shapes.
7. True or false: *Canoso/a, arrugado/a* and *entrado/a en años* are things you would say to describe an elder person.
8. Which of the following adjectives can be used to describe a feminine noun?
   a. Alta
   b. Celeste
   c. Abundante

d. Respingada

9. What's the Spanish word for "mouth"?

10. Choose the odd one out.
    a. Mano

    b. Brazo

    c. Cabello

    d. Dedos.

11. True or false: Possessive articles replace the noun and are used together with a definite article.

12. With which noun do possessive pronouns and adjectives agree? With what they refer to or with the person who owns the thing?

13. Can you name the possessive adjectives equivalent to English "my"?

14. Can you name the definite article that comes before the possessive pronoun *suyos?*

15. Which definite article comes before vuestra?
    a. Los

    b. La

    c. Las

16. True or false: The direct object is the person or thing that receives the action of the verb.

17. With which characteristics of the noun does the direct object pronoun need to agree?

18. Correct the word order in the second sentence: *Tiene un coche nuevo. Compró lo hace poco.*

19. True or false: The indirect object is the person or thing the action is intended to benefit or harm.

20. Which of the following is not an indirect object pronoun?
    a. Le

    b. Les

    c. Os

    d. Las

Chapter 7: Eating Out

Hey, there! It's Sarah. After we visited Seville and spent some days with Julio's family, we stayed in the autonomous community of Andalusia, but this time we went to Malaga, which is a coastal province on the shores of the Mediterranean. We took a train that took us from Seville to Malaga in about two hours.

Malaga is in the Costa del Sol, a region in the south of Spain with coastal towns and one of the most important tourist areas in the whole of Spain. The sun shines more than 320 days a year in this region. Amazing, right?

Here, we wanted to take advantage of the beautiful beaches to simply rest, get in the water and... eat, since Malaga has a great variety of restaurants and bars to visit.

Eating Habits

Did you know that in Spain and Latin American countries, they have four meals a day instead of three? Well, I didn't either, and it blew my mind because we're definitely missing the best one of them all!

Just like in the United States, they have breakfast, lunch, and dinner, which are called *desayuno, almuerzo* (o simplemente, *comida*), and *cena,* respectively. And then, they have the amazing *merienda* – like a big snack in the afternoon. For this meal, you can eat cake, muffins, toast, cookies, waffles, and other snacks, and drink tea, coffee or juice, but in some places, you might also eat a sandwich.

But why do they have an extra meal? Well, in Spain, they have breakfast early in the morning and lunch at about midday, but their dinner is at around 9 p.m. or even later, which means that they are probably hungry at around 5 p.m. – and that's when they decide to have a *merienda*.

Talking about your Favorite Food

Well, as you might have already noticed, I love food. When Julio and I were traveling from Fuengirola to Marbella (two cities in Malaga), we started talking about our favorite foods and what we wanted to eat once we had arrived. The conversation went something like this:

• Mi comida preferida es la paella. ¿Y la tuya, Sarah?	• My favorite food is paella. And yours, Sarah?
○ Uf, es difícil elegir. Mi comida preferida de Estados Unidos son los macarrones con queso.	○ Ugh, it's hard to choose. My favorite food in America is macaroni and cheese.
• ¿Cuál es tu comida española favorita?	• What's your favorite Spanish food?
○ Pues, a mí no me gustó mucho la paella. Lo que más me gustó fue la tortilla de patatas que preparamos.	○ Well, I didn't like paella that much. What I liked the most was the potato tortilla we made.
• ¡Sí! Estaba muy buena.	• Yes! It was very good.
○ ¿Y cuál es tu comida favorita de Estados Unidos?	○ And what's your favorite American food?
• La comida que más me gusta de Estados Unidos son las costillas con salsa barbacoa.	• The food I like the most in the United States is ribs with barbecue sauce.

○ Sí, ¡qué rico! Tanto hablar de comida me dio hambre.	○ Yeah, yummy! So much talk of food made me hungry.
● ¿Qué quieres comer hoy en Marbella?	● What do you want to eat today in Marbella?
○ No sé qué hay, ¿tú qué me recomiendas?	○ I don't know the options, what do you recommend?
● Podríamos ir a comer al restaurante La Milla Marbella que está sobre la playa.	● We could go and eat at La Milla Marbella, a restaurant on the beach.
○ ¿Qué hay allí?	○ What do they serve there?
● Un poco de todo, pero tienen las mejores ostras. También tienen un gazpacho buenísimo.	● A little bit of everything, but they have the best oysters. They also have an amazing gazpacho.
○ Ahora no puedo esperar para llegar. ¡Vayamos!	○ Now I can't wait to get there. Let's go!

Now, I'm going to leave you with Julio so that he can teach you everything he taught me in order to be able to have this conversation!

Hey! It's Julio again! Let's learn how to talk about food – clearly, one of our favorite topics.

To talk about your favorite food, you can use the phrase *Mi comida preferida/favorita es...* ("My favorite food is...") and then add the name of your favorite food. Simple as that!

Expressing Likes/Dislikes

Now, let's move on to talking about our likes and dislikes. To do this, we can use different verbs depending on how much we like or dislike something. We use the verbs *encantar* or *gustar*.

Encantar means "to love" and can be used with people, things, and activities. *Gustar* is the one that is used the most because it is the most "neutral" option. It means "to like" and can also be used with people, things, and activities.

We use *encanta* and *gusta* with singular nouns and verbs, but *encantan* and *gustan* with plural nouns. For example, we can say *Me gusta la paella* and *Me gusta comer paella*, but *Me gustan las ostras.*

You may be wondering what the *me* at the beginning of the example sentences means. Well, unlike other verbs, these verbs need some personal pronouns that are different from the ones we've seen so far. These pronouns are called *pronombres átonos* and, just like with the personal pronouns we already know, their use depends on the person and number of the person we are talking about in the following way:

- 1st person singular: Me encanta/gusta la paella
- 2nd person singular: Te encanta/gusta la paella
- 3rd person singular: Le encanta/gusta la paella
- 1st person plural: Nos encanta/gusta la paella
- 2nd person plural: Os encanta/gusta la paella
- 3rd person plural: Les encanta/gusta la paella

Furthermore, before these personal pronouns, we can add the ones we've seen – before but preceded by *a*. This, however, is only optional.

- 1st person singular: (A mí) me encanta/gusta la paella
- 2nd person singular: (A ti) te encanta/gusta la paella
- 3rd person singular: (A él/ella) le encanta/gusta la paella
- 1st person plural: (A nosotros/nosotras) nos encanta/gusta la paella
- 2nd person plural: (A vosotros/vosotras) os encanta/gusta la paella
- 3rd person plural: (A ellos/ellas) les encanta/gusta la paella

Now, what about dislikes? Well, to say that we don't love or like something, we simply add a *no* before the *pronombre átono*. Let's see how that would look like:

- 1st person singular: (A mí) **no** me encanta/gusta la paella

- 2nd person singular: (A ti) **no** te encanta/gusta la paella

- 3rd person singular: (A él/ella) **no** le encanta/gusta la paella

- 1st person plural: (A nosotros/nosotras) **no** nos encanta/gusta la paella

- 2nd person plural: (A vosotros/vosotras) **no** os encanta/gusta la paella

- 3rd person plural: (A ellos/ellas) **no** les encanta/gusta la paella

Comparatives and Superlatives

Well, you're already almost a pro at talking about your likes and dislikes now. But it's time to talk about comparatives and superlatives to talk about the things we like or dislike more, less, or the most.

In Spanish, we compare adjectives, nouns, and adverbs using the following formulas depending on the relationship between the things we are comparing:

- Superiority: *más* + adjective/noun/adverb + *que*

- Inferiority: *menos* + adjective/noun/adverb + *que*

- Equality: *tan* + adjective/adverb + *como*

Of course, you should always remember that when we compare adjectives, they should always agree in gender and number with the element we are comparing.

For example, we can say *La paella es más sabrosa que la tortilla* ("*Paella* is tastier than *tortilla*"), *La paella es menos sabrosa que la tortilla* ("*Paella* is less tasty than *tortilla*"), and *La paella es tan sabrosa como la tortilla* ("*Paella* is as tasty as *tortilla*").

The only exception to the use of *más* and *menos* are the adjectives *bueno, malo, grande* (when it refers to age), and *pequeño* (when it refers to age), which in the comparative form turn into *mejor, peor, mayor,* and *menor* respectively, instead of *más bueno, más malo, más grande* and *más pequeño.*

If we want to compare nouns with a relationship of equality, we don't use *tan*, but *tanto, tanta, tantos,* or *tantas,* depending on the gender and number of the nouns we are comparing. For example: *No como tantas ostras como patatas fritas.*

We can also compare verbs using the following formula:

- verb + *más que*
- verb + *menos* que
- verb + *tanto* como

For example: *Yo como más que Sarah ("I eat more than Sarah"), Yo como menos que Sarah ("I eat less than Sarah"),* and *Yo como tanto como Sarah ("I eat the same as Sarah").*

Now let's move on to the superlatives. To say that something is at the top or bottom of its class, we use the following formula:

- *el/la/los/las* + *más* + adjective (+ *de* + group)
- *el/la/los/las* + *menos* + adjective (+ *de* + group)

For example: *Esta es la paella más rica del mundo ("This is the tastiest paella in the world"),* or *La paella de este lugar es la menos rica de todas ("The paella of the place is the one I liked the least").*

For this formula, remember that the article choice depends on the gender and the number of the thing we are talking about.

Here's an example sentence to sum up everything we've seen on likes, dislikes, comparatives, and superlatives:

- Me gusta más la paella que la tortilla, pero lo más rico de todo son las ostras ("I like paella more than tortilla, but oysters are what I like the most ").

Types of Meals

Sarah has already told you about the four meals we eat in Spain, but now it's time to see what we might eat at a restaurant for lunch and dinner.

In Spain, the appetizer eaten before the main course is generally called *primeros*, the main course is called *segundos*, and the dessert is called *postre.*

De primero we can have things like *gazpacho, lentejas,* and *tortilla de patatas. De segundo* we can have things like *paella, merluza,* and *lomo.* And *de postre* we can have things like *arroz con leche, fruta,* and *helado.*

91

Ordering Food

Now it's time to learn how to order some food. Here is a list of phrases that would be useful at a restaurant:

- Una mesa para dos, por favor ("A table for two, please")
- ¿Cuál es el menú del día? ("What's today's special?")
- ¿Qué plato me recomienda? ("What dish do you recommend?")
- ¿Qué trae este plato? ("What does this dish have?")
- Soy alérgico a las nueces ("I'm allergic to nuts")
- Yo quiero un gazpacho ("I'd like a gazpacho")
- ¿Me podría traer la cuenta, por favor? ("Could you bring the bill, please?")

We finally went to La Milla Marbella. It was a great sunny day, and the lounge chairs of the restaurant were excellent for enjoying the sun and the view. Here's the conversation we had with the waiter:

■ ¡Buenos días! ¿Serán ustedes dos?	■ Good morning! Is it the two of you?
● Hola, sí, una mesa para dos, por favor.	● Hello, yes, table for two, please.
■ Claro, por aquí.	■ Sure, over here.
(...)	(...)
■ Aquí les dejo el menú.	■ Here's the menu.
○ Muchas gracias.	○ Thank you very much.
(...)	(...)
■ ¿Ya saben qué van a pedir?	■ Do you know what are you going to have?

• Sí. De primero, yo quiero un gazpacho y de segundo el solomillo.	• Yes. As a starter, I want a gazpacho, and as a main, the sirloin.
■ Genial, ¿y usted?	■ Great, and for you?
○ Yo de primero quiero unas ostras y de segundo el lomo.	○ As a starter I want some oysters, and as a main, the loin.
■ Muy bien. ¿Qué desean para beber?	■ Very good. What would you like to drink?
• Yo, un agua mineral.	• For me, a mineral water.
○ Y yo una cerveza.	○ And I'll have a beer.
■ Perfecto, en un momento lo traigo.	■ Perfect, I'll get it in a minute.
• Gracias.	• Thank you.
(...)	(...)
○ Disculpe, ¿podemos ver el menú de postres?	○ Excuse me, can we see the dessert menu?
■ Sí, claro. Aquí tienen.	■ Yes, of course. Here you are.
• Gracias.	• Thank you.
(...)	(...)
■ ¿Les apetece algún postre?	■ Would you like something for dessert?
○ Sí. Queremos un arroz con leche para compartir.	○ Yes. We want milk with rice to share.

• ¿Tiene nueces? Yo soy alérgica.	• Does it have any nuts? I'm allergic.
■ No, no tiene nueces.	■ No, it doesn't have nuts.
• Perfecto. Gracias	• Perfect. Thanks.
■ Claro, ya os lo pongo.	■ Sure, I'll be right back.
○ Gracias.	○ Thank you.
(...)	(...)
• Disculpe, ¿podría traer la cuenta, por favor?	• Excuse, could you bring the bill, please?
■ Claro. ¿Qué tal ha estado la comida?	■ Of course. How was your meal?
• Todo ha estado riquísimo.	• Everything has been delicious.
■ Me alegro. Ya os traigo la cuenta.	■ Happy to hear. I'll bring you the check.

Adverbs of Mode

When we talked about comparatives and superlatives, we also discussed how to compare adverbs. We've already defined them, talked about adverbs of place and quantity, and now it's time to get to some adverbs of mode so that you can use them to compare. Here are some adverbs:

- *Bien* means "well"
- *Mal* means "bad"
- *Mejor* means "better" (remember that it is one of the exceptions of the comparative form with *más*)
- *Peor* means "worse" (remember that it is one of the exceptions of the comparative form with *más*)
- *despacio* means "slowly"

- *rápido* means "fast"
- *deprisa* means "fast"

And there are also other adverbs of mode in Spanish, which are formed with the ending *-mente* and are similar to the English adverbs ending in "-ly." These adverbs are formed with the feminine singular form of adjectives plus the ending *-mente*. Furthermore, these adverbs are an exception to the accent rules because if the adjective has a *tilde*, then the adverb formed with that adjective will maintain that *tilde*.

Here are a few examples of these adverbs:

- *rápidamente* means "fastly"
- *solamente* means "only"
- *difícilmente* means "hardly"
- *claramente* means "clearly"
- *comúnmente* means "commonly"
- *últimamente* means "lately"
- *felizmente* means "happily"
- *tímidamente* means "timidly"
- *simplemente* means "simply"

Conjunctions

Since we're starting to get into more complex sentences, I believe it's high time we see some conjunctions to connect sentences. Conjunctions are words used to join two or more elements or sentences. We've already talked a bit about *y* and *pero,* which mean *and* or *but,* respectively.   Now, let's see some other conjunctions:

- *O:* it means "or"
- *Ni:* it means "neither" or "nor" and is used when we want to add something negative
- *Porque:* it means "because"
- *Aunque:* it means "although"
- *Sin embargo:* it means "however"
- *Como:* it means "as," "since" or "like"
- *Aún:* it means "yet"

- *A pesar de que*: it means "In spite of"
- *Mientras*: it means "while"
- *Cuando*: it means "when"
- *Si*: it means "if"

Exercises

1. True or False: Desayuno and Merienda are the same in Spanish

2. How do you say "My favorite food is spaghetti" in Spanish?

3. True or False: the verbs *encantar* and *gustar* mean exactly the same.

4. To talk about our likes and dislikes, which of these two options do we use with verbs?

    a. encanta

    b. encantan

5. Which of these is the correct form of saying "I like oysters" in Spanish?

    a. Gusta me las ostras

    b. Me gustan las ostras

    c. A mí gustan las ostras

6. And which of these is the correct form of saying "They like paella" in Spanish?

    a. Ellos gustan paella

    b. A ellos gustan paella

    c. A ellos les gusta la paella

7. Which of these is the correct form of saying "He doesn't like eating pasta" in Spanish?

    a. No te gustan comer pasta

    b. No le gusta comer pasta

    c. No gustan comer pasta

8. How do we say "This shirt is smaller than that one" in Spanish?

    a. Esta camisa es más pequeña que aquella

    b. Esta camisa es pequeña que aquella

    c. Está camisa es pequeña como aquella

9. How do we say "I like the table less than the chair" in Spanish?

    a. Me gusta menos la mesa que la silla

    b. Me gusta mejor la mesa que la silla

    c. Me gusta menos la silla que la mesa

10. How do we say "Érica is older than Carlos" in Spanish?

    a. Érica es más grande que Carlos

    b. Érica es más mayor que Carlos

    c. Érica es mayor que Carlos

11. How do we say "This book is worse than the previous one" in Spanish?

    a. Este libro es más malo que el anterior

    b. Este libro es más mejor que el anterior

    c. Este libro es peor que el anterior

12. True or False: In Spain, they call *primeros* to the main course.

13. How do you ask what is in a dish in Spanish?

    a. ¿Cuál es el menú del día?

    b. ¿Qué trae este plato?

    c. ¿Qué plato me recomienda?

14. How would you order a pizza?

15. How would you ask for the bill?

16. What is the Spanish adverb to say "well"?

17. How are adverbs ending in *-mente* formed?

    a. the feminine form of the adjective + *-mente*

    b. the masculine form of the adjective + *-mente*

    c. the plural form of the adjective + *-mente*

18. What does the conjunction *o* mean?

19. To give a reason, which of these conjunctions would we use?

    a. y

    b. como

    c. aún

    d. porque

20. What does the conjunction *si* mean? Is it the same as *sí*?

Chapter 8: Booking Tickets

For one of our last destinations before returning to the US, I wanted to take Sarah to the city with the most Muslim heritage in Spain. Granada was under a Muslim government for 781 years (from 711 to 1492), more than any other Spanish territory. The Alhambra, an Islamic citadel and palace, is one of the most visited monuments in Spain and one of the best-preserved examples of Islamic architecture in the world. It's an amazing place, with many sites worth visiting, like the Nasrid Palaces, the Generalife, the Alcazaba, the Palace of Carlos V, and the Bath of the Mosque.

Besides its amazing architecture and heritage, Granada is famous for having the Mediterranean Sea and the Sierra Nevada mountain range, only 45 minutes away. This means that, on some days, you can go skiing or snowboarding in the morning and you can swim in the ocean in the afternoon. This also means that Granada can get cold in the winter, with temperatures dropping to around 1 °C (34 °F) during the night, and it's warm in the summer months, with temperatures reaching over 40 °C (104 °F).

Booking a Ticket

Julio and I took a bus from Málaga to Granada. It was a two-hour bus ride, and we used that time to book the tickets to visit Alhambra. Since it's a historical site, they limit the number of people that can visit it at the same time. As always, Julio used it as an excuse to teach me some more Spanish.

First of all, we entered the official Alhambra website, and checked the opening and closing times. This is what we found:

16 de marzo a 15 de octubre	March 16th to October 15th
Mañana: de 8:30 a 12:00	Morning: from 8:30 to 12:00 a.m.
Tarde: de 2:00 a 8:00	Afternoon: from 2:00 to 8:00 p.m.
Noche: de 10:00 a 11:30 (de martes a sábado)	Night: from 10:00 to 11:30 p.m. (Tuesday to Saturday)
16 de octubre a 15 de marzo	October 16th to March 15th
Mañana: de 8:30 a 12:00	Morning: from 8:30 to 12:00 a.m.
Tarde: de 2:00 a 6:00	Afternoon: from 2:00 to 6:00 p.m
Noche: de 8:00 a 9:30 (viernes y sábados)	Night: from 8:00 to 9:30 p.m. (Fridays and Saturdays)

With this information, we went to the booking section to see what was available. This is the conversation that we had:

○ Como estamos en verano, la Alhambra está abierta desde las ocho y media de la mañana hasta las ocho de la noche. Y después abre de nuevo a la noche, de diez a once y media. ¿Te gustaría hacer una visita nocturna?	○ As it's the summer, the Alhambra is open from eight thirty in the morning until eight in the evening. And then it opens again at night, from ten to eleven thirty. Would you like to make an evening visit?

• No, prefiero hacer la visita de día, para poder ver mejor.	• No, I prefer to visit it during the day, so I can see better.
○ Sí, estoy de acuerdo. Y creo que lo mejor es ir temprano a la mañana, para evitar el calor, ¿no?	○ Yes, I agree. And I think it's best to go early in the morning, to avoid the heat, right?
• Vale, temprano a la mañana o a última hora de la tarde, cuando baja el sol.	• Okay, early in the morning or late in the afternoon, when the sun goes down.
○ Lo bueno de ir a la tarde es que no tenemos que madrugar.	○ The good thing about going in the afternoon is that we don't have to get up early.
• Sí, después de tanto tiempo viajando ya estoy algo cansada.	• Yeah, after all this time traveling, I'm a little tired.
○ Bien, déjame fijarme si hay entradas disponibles para mañana a la tarde. ¿A qué hora quieres ir, más o menos?	○ Okay, let me see if there are any tickets available for tomorrow afternoon. Around what time do you want to go?
• ¿Qué te parece alrededor de las cinco de la tarde? Así tendremos tiempo de ver todo antes de que cierre.	• What do you think about five o'clock in the afternoon? Then we'll have time to see everything before it closes.
○ Perfecto.	○ Perfect.

Once we decided when we wanted to go, Julio tried to book the tickets online, but the web page wasn't working. So he had this great idea: I was going to call the booking office to buy the tickets over the phone. I wasn't thrilled, but I did it anyways, and this is the dialogue I had with the phone operator:

○ Buenas tardes, se comunicó con la boletería de la Alhambra, ¿en qué puedo ayudarle?	○ Good afternoon, you've reached the Alhambra ticket office, how can I help you?
• Buenas tardes, quería comprar entradas para visitar el complejo.	• Good afternoon, I wanted to buy tickets to visit the complex.
○ Para comprar entradas deberá ingresar a nuestra página web.	○ To buy tickets you will need to access our website.
• Lo sé, pero la página web no anda en este momento. ¿Podrá venderme las entradas por teléfono?	• I know, but the website isn't up and running right now. Can you sell me the tickets over the phone?
○ Bien, como la página no anda, podemos hacer una excepción. ¿Cuántas personas visitarán el complejo?	○ Okay, since the page isn't working, we can make an exception. How many people will visit the complex?
• Seremos dos personas.	• We'll be two people.
○ ¿Dos adultos?	○ Two adults?
• Sí.	• Yes.
○ ¿Cuándo os gustaría venir?	○ When would you like to come?
• Vamos mañana, si quedan entradas. Idealmente, a eso de las cinco de la tarde.	• We'll go tomorrow, if there are tickets available. Ideally, around five in the afternoon.

o Muy bien, hoy es vuestro día de suerte, porque justo quedan dos entradas de adultos para mañana, martes 15, a las 17:00 hs.	o Very good, today is your lucky day, because there are just two adult tickets left for tomorrow, Tuesday 15, at 17:00 hs.
• ¡Qué bien!	• Wonderful!

After that, I gave her my credit card details, and she emailed me the tickets.

Telling the Time/Date

Sarah did a great job booking the tickets over the phone. After that, we talked a bit more about telling the time and date in Spanish.

To tell the time, we use the verb *ser* conjugated in the third person plural of the present tense (that is, *son*). Next, we add the feminine definite article *las*, and finally, we say the part of the day:

- *De la mañana* means "in the morning" or "a.m."
- *De la tarde* means "in the afternoon" or "p.m." We use this after midday.
- *De la noche* means "at night" or "p.m." We use this when it's dark outside.
- *Son las cinco de la tarde* means "It's five p.m."
- *Son las dos de la mañana* means "It's two a.m."
- *Son las nueve de la noche* means "It's nine p.m."

For 1 a.m. and 1 p.m., we use the singular conjugation of the third person in the present tense of the verb *ser* (that is, *es*) followed by the feminine definite article *la* and the part of the day:

- *Es la una de la mañana* means "It's one a.m." We can also say *madrugada* instead of *mañana* for the early hours of the morning: *Es la una de la madrugada*.
- *Es la una de la tarde* means "It's one p.m." Around noon, you can also say *mediodía*: *Son las doce del mediodía* means "It's 12 a.m." or "It's midday."

These are some useful phrases to ask for the time:

- *¿Qué hora es?*, which means "What time is it?"
- *¿Tienes hora?*, which means "Do you have the time?"
- *¿Puedes decirme la hora?*, which means "Can you tell me what's the time?"

Telling the date is quite simple. As a rule of thumb, you can use this formula: Day of the week + number + *de* + month of the year + *de* + year. For example:

Martes tres de marzo de 2020 means "Tuesday, March 3rd, 2020."

To say the date in English, we normally use ordinals ("third," "fifth"). However, in Spanish, we use the cardinals (*tres, cinco*), that is, just the number, except for the first day of the month, in which case we use *primero* ("first"):

Hoy es primero de enero ("Today is January, 1st.")

To be able to say the date correctly, let's go over the days of the week and the months of the year:

Los días de la semana

- *Lunes* means "Monday"
- *Martes* means "Tuesday"
- *Miércoles* means "Wednesday"
- *Jueves* means "Thursday"
- *Viernes* means "Friday"
- *Sábado* means "Saturday"
- *Domingo* means "Sunday"

Los meses del año

- *Enero* means "January"
- *Febrero* means "February"
- *Marzo* means "March"
- *Abril* means "April"
- *Mayo* means "May"
- *Junio* means "June"
- *Julio* means "July"

- *Agosto* means "August"
- *Septiembre* means "September"
- *Octubre* means "October"
- *Noviembre* means "November"
- *Diciembre* means "December"

Another thing worth noting is that, in Spanish, the names of days and months are not capitalized as in English:

- *Hoy es viernes 27 de mayo* ("Today is Friday, May 27th.")
- *Ayer fue jueves 26 de mayo* ("Yesterday was Thursday, May 26th.")
- *Mañana será sábado 28 de mayo* ("Tomorrow will be Saturday, May 28th.")

Ordinal Numbers

In the previous section, we mentioned cardinal and ordinal numbers. Cardinal numbers are the ones we saw in the first chapter: *uno, dos, tres,* and so on and so forth. You already know them. So now we'll focus on ordinal numbers or ordinals, for example, *primero,* which means "first." We can think of them as adjectives made from numbers; like many other Spanish adjectives, they change according to the gender and number of the noun they are modifying. Let's see some examples:

- *Mi cuarta hija irá a la universidad el año que viene* ("My fourth daughter will go to college next year")
- *Los primos segundos de Julio vendrá de visita desde Valencia* ("Julio's second cousins will come to visit from Valencia")

Here's a list of the most common ordinal numbers:

- Primero, primera, primeros, primeras mean "first"
- Segundo and its variants mean "second"
- Tercero and its variants mean "third"
- Cuarto and its variants mean "fourth"
- Quinto and its variants mean "fifth"
- Sexto and its variants mean "sixth"

- Séptimo and its variants mean "seventh"
- Octavo and its variants mean "eighth"
- Noveno and its variants mean "nineth"
- Décimo and its variants mean "tenth"

Another difference between English and Spanish regarding ordinals is that in Spanish, they are less common than in English. We tend to use just the number, especially in oral speech. So, it's common to modify a sentence so that the ordinal is not used (this is especially true for numbers above ten). For example, while in English we talk about "the 21st century," in Spanish, we call it *el siglo XXI* (centuries are normally written in Roman numerals) and not *el siglo vigésimo primero.*

The last thing you need to know about Spanish ordinals is that when *primero* ("first") and *tercero* ("third") are placed before a singular masculine noun, they are shortened to *primer* and *tercer*, respectively. Take a look at these examples:

- *El primer día de clases, los alumnos ingresarán una hora más tarde* ("On the first day of school, students will start an hour later")
- *Guardo los cubiertos en el tercer cajón de la cocina* ("I keep the cutlery in the kitchen third drawer")

Unisex Nouns

By now, you already know that Spanish nouns have gender. Some are always masculine, like *el árbol* ("the tree"), others are always feminine, like *la luz* ("the light"), and there's a third group, normally those referring to people, which change their ending according to whom we are talking about. For example, we say *el enfermero* ("the male nurse") and *la enfermera* ("the female nurse"). However, as always, there are exceptions. Here's a list of nouns that stay the same regardless of who we are talking about. In these cases, we express the gender of the person through the article preceding it:

Masculine	Feminine	Translation
el artista	la artista	the artist
el astronauta	la astronauta	the astronaut
el atleta	la atleta	the athlete
el comentarista	la comentarista	the commentator
el dentista	la dentista	the dentist
el estudiante	la estudiante	the student
el modelo	la modelo	the model
el oficinista	la oficinista	the office worker
el periodista	la periodista	the journalist
el policía	la policía	the police officer

Talking About Future Plans

In this chapter, we spoke about the future. Like in English, we have several ways to refer to the future in Spanish.

We can use the present:

- *Vamos mañana, si quedan entradas* ("We are going tomorrow, if there are tickets left")

- *La semana que viene volvemos a Estados Unidos* ("Next week we get back to the States")

Another option is using the present tense of the verb *ir* followed by the preposition *a* and an infinitive. This is similar to the English "going to" followed by an infinitive:

- *Mañana a las cinco **vamos a visitar** la Alhambra* ("Tomorrow at 5 we are going to visit the Alhambra")

- *Después de unas semanas de vacaciones, pronto **van a volver** a casa* ("After some weeks on holidays, they are going to return home")

A third way of talking about the future is using the future tense.

Future Tenses for Regular / Irregular Verbs

This is the tense we use to talk about things that will happen or that will be true in the future:

- ***Tendremos** tiempo de ver todo antes de que cierre* ("We'll have time to see everything before it's closed")

- *Para comprar entras **deberá** ingresar a nuestra página web* ("To buy tickets you'll need to go to our web page")

- *¿Cuántas personas **visitarán** el complejo?* ("How many people will be visiting the complex?")

As with the other tenses, for regular verbs, we form the future tense by changing the ending. Let's take a look at the conjugation of the three model verbs: *amar, temer,* and *partir.*

	AMAR	TEMER	PARTIR
yo	amaré	temeré	partiré
tú	amarás	temerás	partirás
él / ella	amará	temerá	partirá
nosotros / nosotras	amaremos	temeremos	partiremos
vosotros / vosotras	amaréis	temeréis	partiréis
ellos / ellas / ustedes	amarán	temerán	partirán

Finally, let's also take a look at the future form of some irregular verbs:

	DECIR	HACER	HABER	PONER	TENER	QUERER
yo	diré	haré	habré	pondré	tendré	querré
tú	dirás	harás	habrás	pondrás	tendrás	querrás
él / ella	dirá	hará	habrá	pondrá	tendrá	querrá
nosotros / nosotras	diremos	haremos	habremos	pondremos	tendremos	querremos
vosotros / vosotras	diréis	haréis	habréis	pondréis	tendréis	querréis
ellos / ellas / ustedes	dirán	harán	habrán	pondrán	tendrán	querrán

Choosing a Movie

After visiting the Alhambra, we had some *tapas*: small plates of food served as a snack alongside beer or wine. Luckily, Granada is one of the places in Spain where they still serve them for free with each drink you order. We were exhausted after walking all day, so we decided to watch a movie in our hotel room. Choosing the right one wasn't easy! This is the conversation I had with Julio:

○ Quizás deberíamos ver una película española, ¿o no? Así practicas.	○ Maybe we should watch a Spanish movie, right? So you can practice.
• Sí, es una buena idea. Pero voy a tener que prestar mucha atención y estoy demasiado cansada.	• Yes, that's a good idea. But I'm going to have to pay attention and I'm too tired.

○ Tienes razón, yo también estoy cansado. ¿Qué te parece si vemos una película española con subtítulos?	○ You're right, I'm tired too. What do you say we watch a Spanish movie with subtitles?
● ¡Buena idea! Me gustaría ver la última de Almodóvar, que todavía no la he visto.	● Good idea! I'd like to see Almodóvar's last one, which I haven't seen yet.
○ Yo tampoco la he visto. ¿Esa es la película en la que Penélope Cruz hace de una madre bondadosa y trabajadora, con un marido miserable y borracho?	○ I haven't seen her either. Is that the movie in which Penelope Cruz plays a kind and hardworking mother, with a miserable and drunk husband?
● ¡No, Julio! Esa es Volver, es del 2006. En esta Penélope Cruz hace de madre soltera. Es una mujer determinada que se hace amiga de una joven un poco abandonada por sus propios padres.	● No, Julio! That's "Volver," it's from 2006. In this one, Penelope Cruz plays as a single mother. She's a determined woman who befriends a young woman abandoned by her own parents.
○ Parece interesante. Vale, veámosla.	○ Sounds interesting. Okay, let's watch it.

Adverbs of Affirmation/Negation/Doubt

In the previous dialogue, Sarah and I used some adverbs to express affirmation, negation, and doubt. Here's a list of the ones we used and some others:

Affirmation:

- *Sí* means "yes"
- *Claro* and *por supuesto* mean "of course"
- *En efecto* means "indeed"

109

- *Verdaderamente* means "truly"
- *Cierto* means "true"
- *También* means "too"

Negation:

- *En absoluto* means "not at all"
- *Jamás* and *nunca* mean "never"
- *Tampoco* means "neither"
- *Ni* means "nor"

Doubt:

- *Quizá(s)*, *a lo mejor*, and *tal vez* mean "perhaps," "maybe"
- *Posiblemente* means "possibly"
- *Probablemente* means "probably"
- *Seguramente* means "surely"

Adjectives for Describing People's Personality

Trying to decide which movie to watch, we used some adjectives to describe the character's personalities. Here you have a list of some other Spanish personality adjectives to describe people:

- *Afectivo* means "affectionate"
- *Bondadoso* means "good-natured"
- *Caprichoso* means "whimsical"
- *Cobarde* means "cowardly"
- *Crédulo* means "gullible"
- *Culto* means "cultured"
- *Desgraciado* means "miserable"
- *Despistado* means "absent-minded"
- *Digno* means "dignified"
- *Egoísta* means "selfish"
- *Encantador* means "charming"
- *Engañoso* means "deceitful"
- *Exigente* means "demanding"

- *Fiel* means "loyal"
- *Gracioso* means "funny"
- *Hablador* means "talkative"
- *Humilde* means "humble"
- *Listo* means "clever"
- *Mimado* means "spoiled"
- *Orgulloso* means "prideful"
- *Presumido* means "smug"
- *Reservado* means "reserved"
- *Seguro* means "confident"
- *Sensato* means "sensible"
- *Sensible* means "sensitive"
- *Sincero* means "sincere"
- *Torpe* means "clumsy"
- *Trabajador* means "hard-working"
- *Tranquilo* means "calm"
- *Valiente* means "courageous"

Exercises

1. True or False: *¿Qué hora es?*, *¿Tienes hora?*, and *¿Puedes decirme la hora?* are three ways of asking what's the time.

2. Which of the following means "in the morning"?
   a. *de la noche*
   b. *de la tarde*
   c. *de la mañana*

3. Which of the following mean "in the afternoon"?
   a. *de la noche*
   b. *de la tarde*
   c. *de la mañana*

4. Which of the following mean "at night"?
   a. *de la noche*
   b. *de la tarde*
   c. *de la mañana*

5. How would you say "It's eight a.m."?

6. Choose the right option for saying "It's one a.m."
   a. *Son la una de la mañana*

   b. *Es la una de la mañana*

7. ¿What's the word for "noon"?

8. Can you list the days of the week in Spanish?

9. And now, can you list the month of the year in Spanish?

10. *Hoy es viernes 27 de mayo* means "Today is Friday, May 27th." Can you say the date on which you are reading this in Spanish?

11. Choose the correct ordinal for the cardinal number *cinco*.
    a. *Segundo*

    b. *Quinto*

    c. *Décimo*

12. True or false: In Spanish, ordinal numbers above ten are very frequent.

13. True or false: Unisex nouns are the ones that stay the same regardless of the gender of the person we are referring to.

14. Which of the following is used to talk about the future in Spanish?
    a. The present tense

    b. *ir* + *a* + infinitive

    c. The future

    d. All of the above

15. Can you conjugate the regular verb *gustar* in the future with the pronouns *yo, tú, él, nosotros, vosotros,* and *ellos?*

16. Can you conjugate the regular verb *leer* in the future with the pronouns *yo, tú, ella, nosotras, vosotras,* and *ellas?*

17. Choose the odd one out:
    a. *Tal vez*   b. *Quizá*

    c. *En efecto*

    d. *A lo mejor*

18. True or false: *Sensible* means "sensible."

19. How would you describe someone who is very selfish?

20. Choose a movie that you like and watch. Afterward, complete this chart with the information about the main character:

Nombre:

Edad:

Características positivas:

Características negativas:

Chapter 9: Talking About Your Past

Hi! It's Sarah here again. We've come to our last stop on this trip: the beautiful city of Madrid.

Julio and his family used to live here when he was young. He still has some friends from school here, and they organized a meet-up to see him.   I was lucky enough to go along with him. They spent a lot of time reminiscing about their past, and they got up to date with their current lives and careers.

Everybody was friendly, and I had a great time. Plus, I got to listen to many conversations using the past and talking about jobs. Here is one of the conversations Julio had with his friend Fernanda.

• ¿Recuerdas cuando caminábamos hasta el lago de la Casa de Campo?	• Remember when we walked to the l ake at Casa de Campo?
○ Claro que lo recuerdo. Nos caímos al lago en pleno invierno. Pasamos mucho frío.	○ Of course I remember. We fell into the lake in the middle of winter. We were so cold.

● ¡Sí! ¿Cómo olvidarlo? Fuimos corriendo a nuestras casas a cambiarnos y abrigarnos.	● Yes! How could I forget? We ran to our houses to change and warm up.
○ Pero despúes nos reunimos en tu casa para comer una pizza.	○ But then we met at your house for pizza.
● Cierto, ¡Alguien comió casi una pizza entera!	● Right, someone ate almost a whole pizza!
○ ¡Cierto! Ese fue Juan. Ahora es doctor y vive en Valencia ¿sabías?	○ True! That was Juan. Now he's a doctor and lives in Valencia, did you know?
● No lo sabía. Oí que se casó, ¿verdad?	● I didn't know. I heard he got married, didn't he?
○ Sí, con Sandra. Tienen dos hijas preciosas.	○ Yeah, with Sandra. They have two beautiful daughters.
● Guau… ¿Y tú? ¿A qué te dedicas estos días?	● Wow… What about you? What do you do these days?
○ Bueno, este año renuncié a mi trabajo y comencé una empresa de arquitectura. ¿Y tú?	○ Well, this year I quit my job and started an architecture firm. And you?
● Como sabes, ahora vivo en Estados Unidos. Allí doy clases de español en escuelas.	● As you know, I live in the United States now. There, I teach Spanish in schools.
○ ¿Y te gusta la vida allí?	○ And do you like your life there?

• Sí, me encanta. Por suerte, el clima de Atlanta es muy parecido al clima de aquí, así que no tuve que acostumbrarme a temperaturas más bajas o más altas.	• Yeah, I love it. Fortunately, Atlanta's weather is very similar to the weather here, so I didn't have to get used to lower or higher temperatures.
○ ¡Qué bueno! ¿Hace cuánto que vives allí?	○ That's good! How long have you been living there?
• En septiembre serán cuatro años.	• In September it will be four years.

Seasons

Hey! It's Julio here. Let's talk a bit about seasons since it came up in my conversation with Fernanda, and I realized that you probably don't know them.

The *estaciones* ("seasons") are:

- *verano,* which means "summer," the season we're now.

- *otoño,* which means "fall."

- *invierno,* which means "winter," the season in which my friends and I fall into the lake.

- *primavera,* which means "spring."

You should remember that in Spain, the seasons are simultaneous with the United States or England. However, in many Latin American countries, the opposite happens.

What do I mean? Well, in countries like Argentina, Bolivia, Chile, and Perú, which are in the southern hemisphere, the seasons are opposite of the ones in Spain, England, and the United States. There, it is summer, when in the northern hemisphere, it's winter. Conversely, it's winter in the southern hemisphere when it's summer in the northern hemisphere.

Talking about Past Events: the *Pretérito Perfecto Simple*

Let's see one of the tenses we use to talk about past events. In Spanish, we use the *pretérito perfecto simple* to talk about events that started and finished in the past and have no connection with the present. For example, once we get back to Atlanta, we will be able to say: *Sarah y yo fuimos a España* ("Sarah and I went to Spain").

An example of the *pretérito perfecto simple* in the conversation I had with Fernanda would be the part where we talk about the one time we all fell in the lake. This is because it was a single event that happened in the past and had no relation to the time of our conversation.

Now, let's see the conjugation of this tense.

Here is the conjugation of *amar, temer,* and *partir,* three regular verbs that you can use as models to conjugate other regular verbs ending in -*ar,* -*er,* and -*ir*.

	AMAR	**TEMER**	**PARTIR**
yo	am<u>é</u>	tem<u>í</u>	part<u>í</u>
tú	am<u>aste</u>	tem<u>iste</u>	part<u>iste</u>
él / ella	am<u>ó</u>	tem<u>ió</u>	part<u>ió</u>
nosotros / nosotras	am<u>amos</u>	tem<u>imos</u>	part<u>imos</u>
vosotros / vosotras	am<u>astei s</u>	tem<u>isteis</u>	part<u>isteis</u>
ellos / ellas / ustedes	am<u>aron</u>	tem<u>ieron</u>	part<u>ieron</u>

Note that the conjugation of regular verbs ending in -*er* and -*ir* is the same, making it easier to remember!

Now is a good time to mention that the *pretérito perfecto simple* is the Spanish tense with more irregular verbs. Here are some of the most used irregular verbs:

	SER/IR	ESTAR	HABER	TRAER	TENER
yo	fui	estuve	hube	traje	tuve
tú	fuiste	estuviste	hubiste	trajiste	tuviste
él / ella	fue	estuvo	hubo	trajo	tuvo
nosotros / nosotras	fuimos	estuvimos	hubimos	trajimos	tuvimos
vosotros / vosotras	fuisteis	estuvisteis	hubisteis	trajisteis	tuvisteis
ellos / ellas / ustedes	fueron	estuvieron	hubieron	trajeron	tuvieron

The verbs *ser* and *ir* are in the same column because their *pretérito perfecto simple* conjugation is the same. Weird right? But also true. We know which one we're talking about, depending on the context.

Talking about childhood habits: *the pretérito imperfecto*

The English simple past can be translated into Spanish as two tenses, the *pretérito perfecto simple*, which we've talked about in the previous section, and the *pretérito imperfecto*, which is the one we're going to talk about now. Why two tenses? Well, as we've mentioned, the *pretérito perfecto simple* is used to talk about single events in the past, which is something for which we'd use the present simple. While the *pretérito imperfecto* is used to talk about habits or actions that used to happen in the past and have no temporal limits, which is something for which we'd also use the present simple in English.

For example, in my conversation with Fernanda, she mentioned *¿Recuerdas cuando caminábamos hasta el lago?* In this sentence, *caminábamos hasta el lago* is in the *pretérito imperfecto* tense because it's something that we used to do a lot when we were kids.

Let's see the regular conjugations of this tense:

	AMAR	TEMER	PARTIR
yo	am<u>aba</u>	tem<u>ía</u>	part<u>ía</u>
tú	am<u>abas</u>	tem<u>ías</u>	part<u>ías</u>
él / ella / usted	am<u>aba</u>	tem<u>ía</u>	part<u>ía</u>
nosotros / nosotras	am<u>ábamos</u>	tem<u>íamos</u>	part<u>íamos</u>
vosotros / vosotras	am<u>abais</u>	tem<u>íais</u>	part<u>íais</u>
ellos / ellas / ustedes	am<u>aban</u>	tem<u>ían</u>	part<u>ían</u>

In this tense, the conjugations of the regular verbs ending in *-er* and *-ir* are also the same. Moreover, the conjugations of the first- and third-person singular are also the same for every verb!

Now, let's see the conjugations of some irregular verbs:

	SER	VER	IR
yo	era	veía	iba
tú	eras	veías	ibas
él / ella / usted	era	veía	iba
nosotros / nosotras	éramos	veíamos	íbamos

vosotros / vosotras	erais	veías	ibais
ellos / ellas / ustedes	eran	veían	iban

As you can see, even in the conjugation of the irregular verbs, the first- and third-person singular are the same for every verb.

Time Expressions for Past Events

Now it's time to see some time expressions we use with these verbs. When you see one of these time expressions, you will most generally find that there is a past tense following it.

For the *pretérito perfecto simple*, we can use time expressions such as:

- *Ayer,* which means "yesterday"
- *Anoche,* which means "last night"
- *El año pasado,* which means "last year"
- *La semana pasada,* which means "last week"
- *El mes pasado,* which means "last month"
- *Hace días,* which means "days ago"
- *El otro día,* which means "the other day"

We can also use the *pretérito perfecto simple with specific dates, months, or years.*

For the *pretérito imperfecto,* we can use time expressions such as:

- *A los* + age, which means "when I was…" + age
- *Cuando tenía* + age, which means "When I was…" + age
- *Antes,* which means "before"
- *En aquella época,* which means "at that time"
- *Entonces,* which means "back then"
- *Cuando era niño/joven,* which means "when I was a kid/young"

Now I will transcribe another piece of my conversation with Fernanda in which we used some of these expressions and the two different past tenses we've seen so that you can see it all in use!

• En aquella época andábamos mucho en bicicleta. Nos encontrábamos en plaza Mayor y luego íbamos hasta el lago.	• At that time we rode bikes a lot. We used to meet in Plaza Mayor and then we went to the lake.
○ Sí, lo recuerdo. A los 15 años estábamos muy en forma. Ahora no puedo ni andar en bicicleta ni correr.	○ Yes, I remember. When we were 15, we were in great shape. Now I can't ride a bike nor run.
• Pues yo estoy igual. El año pasado comencé a ir al gimnasio, pero no me gustó nada. Cuando era joven disfrutaba de hacer ejercicio.	• Yeah, me neither. Last year I started going to the gym, but I didn't like it at all. When I was young I enjoyed exercising.
○ Sí, yo también. Jugaba mucho al fútbol... Oye, ¿fuiste a la reunión del año pasado? Me contó Joaquín que jugaron al fútbol.	○ Yes, me too. I used to play soccer a lot... Hey, did you go to last year's reunion? Joaquin told me they played soccer.
• Ah, ¡sí! Jugué fatal, pero participé.	• Oh, yes! I played awful, but I took part.
○ Nadie juega bien a esta edad. Ya no es como era antes.	○ Nobody plays well at this age. It's not like it used to be.
• Eso es cierto.	• That's true.

Indefinite Pronouns

Indefinite pronouns are words used to talk about people or things or express some quantity in a vague or general way. Examples of indefinite pronouns in English are "all," "none," "any," etc. For example, in the previous piece of conversation I transcribed for you, I told Fernanda, "Nadie juega bien a esta edad." In this example, "nadie" is an indefinite pronoun that means "nobody" or "no one" and refers vaguely to people in general.

These pronouns are useful in almost any conversation when trying to refer to someone or something that has already been mentioned or can be understood in context. Some of them need to agree on gender, some need to agree in number, and some need to agree in gender and number with the referred person or object.

There are two types of indefinite pronouns in Spanish. The first group is made up of pronouns that are always indefinite, and the second group is made of words that only function as indefinite pronouns when a noun does not follow them.

The ones that are always indefinite pronouns are:

- *nadie,* which means "nobody" and doesn't need to agree in gender nor number.
- *alguien,* which means "someone" and doesn't need to agree in gender nor number.
- *nada,* which means "nothing" and doesn't need to agree in gender nor number.
- *algo,* which means "something" and doesn't need to agree in gender nor number.
- *quienquiera,* which means "whoever" and needs to agree in number. When it is plural, it becomes *quienesquiera.*

The ones that sometimes function as indefinite pronouns are:

- *todo,* which means "everything," "everybody" or "all" and needs to agree in gender and number by changing its ending: *toda, todos, todas.*
- *Mucho,* which means "a lot" or "many" and needs to agree in gender and number by changing its ending: *mucha, muchos, muchas.*
- *Poco,* which means "a little," "few" and needs to agree in gender and number by changing its ending: *poca, pocos, pocas.*
- *Má,s* which means "more" and doesn't need to agree in gender nor number.
- *Meno,s* which means "less" and doesn't need to agree in gender nor number.

- *Alguno,* which means "some" or "a," and needs to agree in gender and number by changing its ending: *alguna, algunos, algunas.*

- *Otro,* which means "another" and needs to agree in gender and number by changing its ending: *otra, otros, otras.*

- *Ninguno,* which means "none"

- *Cualquiera,* which means "any" and doesn't need to agree in gender nor number.

- *Bastante,* which means "some," "quite"

- *Demasiado,* which means "too" and needs to agree in gender and number by changing its ending: *demasiada, demasiados, demasiadas.*

- *Uno,* which means "one" and needs to agree in gender and number by changing its ending: *una, unos, unas.*

- *Demás,* which means "the rest" and doesn't need to agree in gender nor number.

- *Cada,* which means "every" and doesn't need to agree in gender nor number.

Relative Pronouns

Now that we've seen the indefinite pronouns, we should see the relative pronouns as well. Relative pronouns are used to introduce relative clauses, that is, clauses that add information about an element of the principal clause. For example, we could say *La taza que rompí era de vidrio* ("The cup I broke was made of glass"). In this sentence, the clause *"que rompí"* is a relative clause that adds information about the cup, and the relative pronoun, in this case, is *que.*

Que isn't the only relative pronoun in Spanish. There are actually many and which one we use depends on what we are talking about:

- If we want to talk about a person or thing, we can use the relative pronouns:
  - *Que,* which means "that." For example: *La silla que compré ayer es rosa* ("The chair I bought yesterday is pink")

- *el que, la que, los que,* or *las que,* which mean "who" or "that" and need to agree in gender and number with the person or thing we are talking about. For example: *La silla en la que estoy sentada es rosa* ("The chair that I'm sitting in is pink").

- *el cual, la cual, los cuales* or *las cuales* which mean "which" and need to agree in gender and number with the person or thing we are talking about. For example: *La silla en la cual estoy sentada es rosa* ("The chair in which I'm sitting is pink")

- If we want to talk about a person, we can also use the relative pronouns *quien* and *quienes* which mean "who" or "whom" and need to agree in number with the person or persons we're talking about. For example: *Mis amigos, a quienes conocí en el colegio, son españoles* ("My friends, whom I met at school, are Spanish")

- If we want to talk about possession, in English, we use "whose," but in Spanish, we use *cuyo, cuya, cuyos,* or *cuyas,* depending on the gender and number of the thing we are talking about. For example: *La silla, cuyas patas están rotas, es rosa* ("The chair, whose legs are broken, is pink")

- If we want to talk about an amount, we can use the pronouns *cuanto, cuanta, cuantos,* or *cuantas* which mean "those," "all those" or "everything." For example: *Hace todo cuanto le pido* ("He does everything I ask him to do")

Remember that though some of these pronouns are similar to the interrogative pronouns, these are never written with a graphic accent, while the interrogative pronouns always do.

Jobs/Professions

Now it's time to talk about jobs. When I met my friends from school, we had a lot of catching up to do, so many of us talked about our current and old jobs and other people's jobs (as you already saw in my conversation with Fernanda).

Before we get into how to describe jobs and professions, we need to know some jobs and occupations in Spanish, right? Here's a list with a few examples:

- *estudiante* means "student"
- *arquitecto/arquitecta* means "architect"
- *ingeniero/ingeniera* means "engineer"
- *abogado/abogada* means "lawyer"
- *enfermero/enfermera* means "nurse"
- *doctor/doctora* means "doctor"
- *mecánico/mecánica* means "mechanic"
- *cocinero/cocinera* means "cook"
- *mesero/mesera* means "waiter"
- *bombero/bombera* means "firefighter"
- *profesor/profesora* means "teacher
- *pintor/pintora* means "painter"
- *actor/actriz* means "actor/actress"
- *cantante* means "singer"
- empresario/empresaria means "business person"
- *secretario/secretaria* means "secretary"
- *artista* means "artist"
- *contador/contadora* means "accountant"
- *policía* means "police officer"
- *dentista* means "dentist"
- *periodista* means "journalist"
- *traductor/traductora* means "translator"
- *veterinario/veterinaria* means "vet"

Describe Someone's Job

Now it's time to learn how to describe a job. To do so, we can talk about where we work, who we work with, how many hours we work, what we usually do, and our opinion of the job.

For example, I could say: *Por las mañanas trabajo en un colegio secundario enseñando español a niños y por la tarde doy clases de español para adultos en un centro comunitario. A veces el trabajo es difícil, pero nunca es aburrido ni repetitivo.* ("In the morning, I work at a secondary school teaching Spanish to kids, and in the afternoon, I teach Spanish for adults at a community center. Sometimes it's a difficult job, but it's never boring nor repetitive").

We've already learned the exact words to say all of this in Spanish; we just have to put them together:

- To talk about where we work, we use the preposition *en;* for example: *Trabajo en un banco ("I work in a bank").*

- To talk about who we work with, we use the preposition *con;* for example: *Trabajo con clientes ("I work with clients").*

- To talk about our working hours, we can use phrases such as *Trabajo a la mañana, trabajo a la tarde,* or *trabajo de noche ("I work in the morning/afternoon/evening").* We can also specify the hours in which we work, for example: *Trabajo de 9 de la mañana a 7 de la tarde ("I work from 9 a.m. to 7 p.m.").*

- To say what we usually do, we use the present form. Some verbs that we can use are:
  - *vender:* "to sell"
  - *llamar:* "to call"
  - *comprar:* "to buy"
  - *supervisar:* "to supervise"
  - *conducir:* "to drive"
  - *escribir:* "to write"
  - *escuchar:* "to listen"

- Finally, to give our opinion on our job, we might use different adjectives, such as:
  - *entretenido:* "entertaining"
  - *divertido:* "fun"
  - *bien pagado:* "well-paid"
  - *mal pagado:* "badly paid"
  - *estresante:* "stressful"
  - *difícil:* "difficult"

- *demandante*: "demanding"
- *enriquecedor*: "enriching"
- *repetitivo*: "repetitive"
- *aburrido*: "boring"

Sarah has written the following text about her job to practice:

Soy contadora en una empresa internacional de tecnología.	I'm an accountant at an international tech company.
Trabajo todos los días de 8 de la mañana a 5 de la tarde.	I work every day from 8 a.m. to 5 p.m.
En la oficina, trabajo con mucha gente divertida.	At the office, I work with a lot of fun people.
Mi trabajo es difícil, pero también es bien pagado.	My job is hard, but it's also well paid.
Para algunos es aburrido, pero en mi opinión es muy divertido.	For some it's boring, but in my opinion it's a lot of fun.
A veces puede ser estresante.	Sometimes it can be stressful.

Exercises

Now it's time to practice everything we've seen in this chapter, which covers a lot of information.

1. Which season comes before *primavera*? And which one before *otoño*?

2. What do we use the *pretérito perfecto simple* for?

    a. to talk about past habits

    b. to talk about past events

3. True or false: the first person singular and the third person singular conjugations of the *pretérito perfecto simple* are the same.

4. True or false: the *pretérito perfecto simple* conjugations of *ser* and *ir* are the same.

5. What do we use the *pretérito imperfecto* for?

    a. to talk about past habits

    b. to talk about past events

6. True or false: the ending of the conjugations for regular verbs ending in -*er* and -*ir* are the same in the *pretérito perfecto simple* and in the *pretérito imperfecto*.

7. What is the *pretérito imperfecto* conjugation of the second person singular of the verb *amar*?

    a. amabas

    b. amaban

    c. amaron

    d. amaste

8. If I want to talk about one time I got sunburnt at the beach, should I use the *pretérito perfecto simple* or the *pretérito imperfecto*?

9. If I want to talk about how I used to travel around the country with my parents when I was young, should I use the *pretérito perfecto simple* or the *pretérito imperfecto*?

10. What is the *pretérito perfecto simple* conjugation of *estar* in the first person plural?

    a. fuimos

    b. estuvimos

    c. estuvieron

    d. estábamos

11. With which tense do we usually use the time expression *el año pasado*?

12. With which tense do we usually use the time expression *antes*?

13. Which tense do we usually use these time expressions with? There is one that doesn't belong to this group. Which is it?

    a. Entonces

    b. cuando era joven

    c. hace días

    d. a los 14 años

14. What does the indefinite pronoun *nada* mean?

    a. nobody

    b. somebody

    c. everything

    d. nothing

15. What does the indefinite pronoun *ninguno* mean?

    a. many

    b. everybody

    c. none

    d. nobody

16. Does the relative pronoun *el cual* need to agree in gender and number with the thing or person it refers to?

17. Which relative pronouns do we use to talk about possession?

18. How would you say "the places that I visited in Spain are beautiful" in Spanish?

    a. Los lugares que visité en España son hermosos.

    b. Los lugares cuyo visité en España son hermosos.

    c. Los lugares el cual visité en España son hermosos.

    d. Los lugares quienes visité en España son hermosos.

19. How do you say "business person" in Spanish?

    a. cantante

    b. actriz/actor

    c. periodista

    d. empresario/a

20. Which preposition do we use to talk about the place we work at?

    a. *por*

    b. *con*

    c. *en*

    d. de

Chapter 10: Basic Grammar Revision

Hey! It's Julio here again and for the last time. Our journey through my beautiful country has ended, and Sarah and I will be arriving home soon; we're on our plane right now. So we thought we'd go over every grammar topic we've seen throughout this journey over our flight. We encourage you to revise with us! Plus, at the end of this chapter, you will find another quiz to see how you've done this last half of the book.

Let's start our revision!

Word Order

- The most common word order for affirmative sentences is:
  - Noun/Pronoun + Adjective + Verb + Complement + Adverb
- The most common word order for negative sentences is:
  - Noun/Pronoun + Adjective + *no* + Verb + Complement + Adverb
- The most common word order for yes/no questions is:
  - ¿ + Noun/Pronoun + Adjective + Verb + Complement + Adverb + ?

You should remember that in Spanish, the subject can be dropped from the sentence, so it isn't always necessary to mention the noun/pronoun or the adjective that describes the thing/person we're talking about.

Subject Pronouns

- First-person singular: *yo* ("I")
- Second-person singular: *tú* / usted ("you")
- Third-person singular: *él* / *ella* ("he" / "she")
- First-person plural: *nosotros* / *nosotras* ("we")
- Second-person plural: *vosotros* / *vosotras* / *ustedes* ("you")
- *Third-person plural: ellos* / *ellas* ("they")

Keep in mind that the pronouns need to agree with the gender of the person we're talking about

Remember that *usted* is the formal version of *tú,* and that *ustedes* is mostly used in Latin American countries, while *vosotros* and *vosotras* are used mostly in Spain.

Gender of Nouns and Adjectives

In Spanish, every noun has one of two genders: masculine or feminine. Some words are inherently feminine, and some words are inherently masculine. Generally speaking (and especially when we're talking about people), we distinguish feminine from masculine nouns because of their endings:

- Feminine words usually end in -*a*
- Masculine words usually end in -*o*

Usually, with people, we can choose between ending a word with -*a* to talk about a woman or -*o* to talk about a man. For example: *la mexicana* and *el mexicano.* However, there are also some nouns (referring to people) that remain unchanged, for example *la artista* and *el artista.* In these cases, we can tell whether we are talking about a man or a woman if we pay attention to the words surrounding the noun, like the articles and adjectives, which, as you may remember, need to agree in gender with the noun they are referring to.

To make adjectives agree with the noun we're talking about, we usually need to decide whether to end the adjective with an -*a* if the noun is feminine (e.g., *linda)* and -*o* if the noun is masculine (e.g., *lindo)*, but we can also find some invariable adjectives as well (e.g., inteligente).

Number of Nouns and Adjectives

The rules for the pluralization of nouns and adjectives in Spanish are:

- If the singular form ends in a vowel, you need to add an *-s* at the end.
  - Examples: *mesa → mesas, casa → casas, mono → monos, pelota → pelotas*
- If the singular form ends in a consonant or with a stressed vowel, you need to add *-es* at the end.
  - Examples: *ataúd → ataúdes, iglú → iglúes, rey → reyes, pared → paredes*
- If the singular form ends with Z, you need to add *-ces* at the end.
  - Examples: *pez → peces, voz → voces, nuez → nueces, lápiz → lápices*

Remember that in Spanish, adjectives, articles, and verbs need to agree in number with the noun we're talking about.

Definite and Indefinite Articles

Spanish has four variations for the definite articles and four variations for the indefinite articles. They vary according to the gender and number of the noun we're talking about, just like we said before.

The definite and indefinite articles in Spanish are:

	Masculine		Feminine	
	Singulaar	Plural	Singular	Plural
Definite	*El*	*Los*	*La*	*Las*
Indefinite	*Un*	*Unos*	*Una*	*Unas*
Neuter	*Lo*			

Demonstrative Pronouns and Articles

Demonstrative pronouns are words used instead of nouns to point at people or things. There are 15 Spanish demonstrative pronouns in Spanish, while in English, there are only four. This difference is because, in Spanish, we need to consider the gender, number, and distance from the speaker and addressee of the noun it's replacing.

These are the 15 Spanish demonstrative pronouns:

	Masculine		Feminine		Neuter
	Singular	Plural	Singular	Plural	Singular
Object close to the speaker	esto	estos	esta	estas	esto
Object close to the addressee	ese	eso	esa	esas	eso
Object far from both	aquel	aquellos	aquella	aquellas	aquello

133

Interrogative Pronouns

Remember that, in Spanish, all interrogative pronouns take a graphic accent. They are:

- *qué* is used in the same way as English "what?"
- *por qué* is similar to English "why?"
- *cuál* and *cuáles* are the singular and plural equivalents of the English "which?"
- *quién* and *quiénes* are the singular and plural equivalents of "who?"
- *cuánto* and *cuánta* are the masculine and feminine equivalents of "how much?"
- *cuántos* and *cuántas* are the masculine and feminine equivalents of "how many?"
- *dónde* is used in the same way as English "where?"
- *cómo* is used in the same way as "how?"
- *cuándo* is similar to English "when?"

Possessive Adjectives and Pronouns

Possessive adjectives and pronouns are the words we use to show that something belongs to someone. While possessive adjectives go together with the noun, possessive pronouns replace the noun. In Spanish, possessive pronouns and adjectives agree with what they describe (not with the person who owns the thing). And, as you can see, possessive pronouns go together with a definite article, which also needs to agree with the gender of the thing owned.

The Spanish possessive adjectives are:

	Singular		Plural	
	Masculine	Feminine	Masculine	Feminine
"My" (belonging to me)	*Mi*	*Mi*	*Mis*	*Mis*
"Your" (belonging to someone you address as *tú*)	*Tu*	*Tu*	*Tus*	*Tus*
"His," "her," "its," "your" (belonging to someone you address as *usted*)	*Su*	*Su*	*Sus*	*Sus*
"Our" (belonging to us)	*Nuestro*	*Nuestra*	*Nuestros*	*Nuestras*
"Your" (belonging to people you address as *vosotros/vosotras*)	*Vuestro*	*Vuestra*	*Vuestros*	*Vuestras*

"Their," "your" (belonging to people you address as *ustedes*)	*Su*	*Su*	*Sus*	*Sus*

The Spanish possessive pronouns (with their articles) are:

	Singular		Plural	
	Masculine	Feminine	Masculine	Feminine
"Mine" (belonging to me)	*El mío*	*La mía*	*Los míos*	*Las mías*
"Yours" (belonging to someone you address as *tú*)	*El tuyo*	*La tuya*	*Los tuyos*	*Las tuyas*
"His," "hers," "its," "yours" (belonging to someone you address as *usted*)	*El suyo*	*La suya*	*Los suyos*	*Las suyas*
"Ours" (belonging to us)	*El nuestro*	*La nuestra*	*Los nuestros*	*Las nuestras*

"Yours" (belonging to people you address as *vosotros/ vosotras*)	*El vuestro*	*La vuestra*	*Los vuestros*	*Las vuestras*
"Theirs," "yours" (belonging to people you address as *ustedes*)	*El suyo*	*La suya*	*Los suyos*	*Las suyas*

Objective Pronouns

The direct object can be replaced by a pronoun, in which case we put it before the verb. In Spanish, that pronoun needs to agree in gender and number with the noun that's being replaced in the following way:

	Masculine	Feminine
"Me" (first person singular)	*Me*	*Me*
"You" (second person singular *tú*)	*Te*	*Te*
"Him," "her," "it" (third person singular); "you" (second person singular *usted*)	*Lo*	*La*
"Us" (first person plural)	*Nos*	*Nos*

"You" (second person plural *vosotros/vosotras*)	*Os*	*Os*
"Them" (third person plural); "you" (second person plural *ustedes*)	*Los*	*Las*

The indirect object can also be replaced by a pronoun when the person or thing that the action is intended to benefit or harm is understood from the context. In these cases, we use one of the following indirect object pronouns depending on the person and number:

"Me," "to me," "for me" (first person singular)	*Me*
"You," "to you," "for you" (second person singular *tú*)	*Te*
"Him/Her/It," "to him/her/it," "for him/her/it" (third person singular); "You," "to you," "for you" (second person singular *usted*)	*Le*
"Us," "for us," "to us" (first person plural)	*Nos*
"You," "to you," "for you" (second person plural *vosotros/vosotras*)	*Os*

"Them," to them," "for them" (third person plural); "you," "to you," "for you" (second person plural *ustedes*)	*Les*

Expressing Likes and Dislikes

To express likes, we can use the following phrases:

- 1st person singular: (A mí) me encanta/gusta la paella
- 2nd person singular: (A ti) te encanta/gusta la paella
- 3rd person singular: (A él/ella) le encanta/gusta la paella
- 1st person plural: (A nosotros/nosotras) nos encanta/gusta la paella
- 2nd person plural: (A vosotros/vosotras) os encanta/gusta la paella
- 3rd person plural: (A ellos/ellas) les encanta/gusta la paella
- And to express dislikes, we can use the following phrases:
- 1st person singular: (A mí) **no** me encanta/gusta la paella
- 2nd person singular: (A ti) **no** te encanta/gusta la paella
- 3rd person singular: (A él/ella) **no** le encanta/gusta la paella
- 1st person plural: (A nosotros/nosotras) **no** nos encanta/gusta la paella
- 2nd person plural: (A vosotros/vosotras) **no** os encanta/gusta la paella
- 3rd person plural: (A ellos/ellas) **no** les encanta/gusta la paella

Remember that we use *encanta* and *gusta* with singular nouns and verbs, but *encantan* and *gustan* with plural nouns.

Comparatives and Superlatives of Adjectives

In Spanish, we compare adjectives, nouns, and adverbs using the following formulas depending on the relationship between the things we are comparing:

- Superiority: *más* + adjective/noun/adverb + *que*
- Inferiority: *menos* + adjective/noun/adverb + *que*
- Equality: *tan* + adjective/adverb + *como*

We can also compare verbs using the following formula:

- verb + *más que*
- verb + *menos* que
- verb + *tanto* como

To say that something is at the top or bottom of its class, i.e. that it is a superlative, we use the following formula:

- *el/la/los/las* + *más* + adjective (+ *de* + group)
- *el/la/los/las* + *menos* + adjective (+ *de* + group)

For this formula, remember that the article choice depends on the gender and number of the thing we are talking about.

Indefinite Pronouns

Indefinite pronouns are words used to talk about people or things or to express some quantity in a vague or general way.

Here's a list of indefinite pronouns:

- *nadie* means "nobody" and doesn't need to agree in gender nor number.
- *alguien* means "someone" and doesn't need to agree in gender nor number.
- *nada* means "nothing" and doesn't need to agree in gender nor number.
- *algo* means "something" and doesn't need to agree in gender nor number.
- *quienquiera* means "whoever" and needs to agree in number. When it is plural, it becomes *quienesquiera*.
- *todo* means "everything," "everybody" or "all" and needs to agree in gender and number by changing its ending: *toda, todos, todas*.
- *mucho* means "a lot" or "many" and needs to agree in gender and number by changing its ending: *mucha, muchos, muchas*.

- *poco* means "a little," "few" and needs to agree in gender and number by changing its ending: *poca, pocos, pocas.*

- *más* means "more" and doesn't need to agree in gender nor number.

- *menos* means "less" and doesn't need to agree in gender nor number.

- *alguno* means "some" or "a," and needs to agree in gender and number by changing its ending: *alguna, algunos, algunas.*

- *otro* means "another" and needs to agree in gender and number by changing its ending: *otra, otros, otras.*

- *ninguno* means "none."

- *cualquiera* which means "any" and doesn't need to agree in gender nor number.

- *bastante* means "some," "quite"

- *demasiado* means "too" and needs to agree in gender and number by changing its ending: *demasiada, demasiados, demasiadas.*

- *uno* means "one" and needs to agree in gender and number by changing its ending: *una, unos, unas.*

- *demás* means "the rest" and doesn't need to agree in gender nor number.

- *cada* means "every" and doesn't need to agree in gender nor number.

Relative pronouns

Relative pronouns are used to introduce relative clauses, that is, clauses that add information about an element of the principal clause.

- If we want to talk about a person or thing, we can use the relative pronouns:
  - *que* means "that."
  - *el que, la que, los que,* or *las que* which mean "who" or "that" and need to agree in gender and number with the person or thing we are talking about.

- *el cual, la cual, los cuales* or *las cuales* which mean "which" and need to agree in gender and number with the person or thing we are talking about.

- If we want to talk about a person, we can also use the relative pronouns *quien* and *quienes* which mean "who" or "whom" and need to agree in number with the person or persons we're talking about.

- If we want to talk about possession, in English, we use "whose," but in Spanish, we use *cuyo, cuya, cuyos,* or *cuyas,* depending on the gender and number of the thing we are talking about.

- If we want to talk about an amount, we can use the pronouns *cuanto, cuanta, cuantos,* or *cuantas* which mean "those," "all those" or "everything."

Present, Future, and Past Forms of Regular Verbs

Let's go over the different ways in which we can talk about the present, the future, and the past.

- Present: we use the present tense to talk about things that are generally true. We can also talk about the present progressive with the verbal phrase *estar* + gerund.

- Future: we use the future tense to talk about things that will happen in the future. And we can also talk about the future with the present tense and the verbal phrase *ir* + infinitive

- Past: We use the *pretérito perfecto simple* to talk about single events that happened in the past. And we use the *pretérito imperfecto* to talk about habits in the past or things that used to be a certain way in the past.

Here's a chart with the regular conjugations of the different tenses we've seen so far:

	Infinitivo	Presente	Futuro	Pretérito perfecto simple	Pretérito imperfecto
yo	-ar	-o	-aré	-é	-aba
	-er		-eré	-í	-ía
	-ir		-iré		
tú	-ar	-as	-arás	-aste	-abas
	-er	-es	-erás	--iste	-ías
	-ir		-irás		
él / ella / usted	-ar	-a	-ará	-ó	-aba
	-er	-e	-erá	-ió	-ía
	-ir		-irá		
nosotros / nosotras	-ar	-amos	-aremos	-amos	-ábamos
	-er	-emos	-eremos	-imos	-íamos
	-ir	-imos	-iremos		
vosotros /	-ar	-áis	-aréis	-asteis	-abais

vosotras	-er	-éis	-créis	-isteis	-ían
	-ir	-ís	-iréis		
ellos / ellas / ustedes	-ar	-an	-arán	-aron	-aban
	-er	-en	-erán	-ieron	-ían
	-ir		-irán		

Present progressive

Remember that we've also seen the present progressive tense, which is conveyed by the verbal phrase formed by the conjugation of *estar* + gerund.

In Spanish, gerunds are never conjugated and are formed in the following way:

- Infinitive verbs ending in -*ar* end in -*ando* in the gerund.
- Infinitive verbs ending in -*ir* or -*er* end in -*iendo* in the gerund.

Estar is an irregular verb in almost every tense, so this is its conjugation:

	Presente	Futuro	Pretérito perfecto simple	Pretérito imperfecto
yo	estoy	estaré	estuve	estaba
tú	estás	estarás	estuviste	estabas
él / ella / usted	está	estará	estuvo	estaba

nosotros / nosotras	estamos	estaremos	estuvimos	estábamos
vosotros / vosotras	estáis	estaréis	estuvisteis	estabais
ellos / ellas / ustedes	están	estarán	estuvieron	estaban

Ir + infinitive

We use this verbal phrase to talk about the future much the same as we do in the English "going to." To do so, we must conjugate the verb *ir* in the present. Since *ir* is an irregular verb, here's its conjugation in the present:

	IR
yo	voy
tú	vas
él / ella / usted	va
nosotros / nosotras	vamos
vosotros / vosotas	vais
ellos / ellas / ustedes	van

Quiz

Now that we're done revising, it's time for a quiz on the last five chapters so that you test your knowledge. Like in the previous quiz, each right answer is worth one point.

Ready? Let's do it!

1. If I say *Julia es la hermana de mi mamá, la madre de mi prima y la esposa de mi tío*, then who is Julia to me in Spanish?

2. How would you describe your face?

3. What would be the Spanish equivalents to the parts of the body mentioned in the song "head and shoulders, knees and toes"?

4. What are the four possessive pronouns of the first-person with their articles?

5. What is the direct object pronoun for the first person singular masculine and feminine?

6. What is the indirect object pronoun for the third person plural?

7. How would you say "I like *lentejas*, but I don't love *gazpacho*" in Spanish?

8. How would you say "This is the best *paella* in the world" in Spanish?

9. How do you ask for a table for four in Spanish?

10. Which adverb can be formed with the adjective *difícil*?

11. How would you say "Today is Sunday, July 18th, 2021" in Spanish?

12. Can you conjugate the regular verb *cantar* in the future tense with the pronouns *yo, tú, ella, nosotras, vosotras,* and *ellas*?

13. How would you say "Tomorrow we are going to sing all night" in Spanish using the verbal phrase *ir +* infinitive?

14. Is *en absoluto* an adverb of affirmation, negation, or doubt? What does it mean?

15. If a man is *torpe*, what is he?

16. What is the difference between the *pretérito perfecto simple* and the *pretérito imperfecto*? What are each of them used for?

17. Can you conjugate the regular verb *salir* in the *pretérito perfecto simple* with the pronouns *yo, tú, él, nosotros,*

vosotros, and *ellos?*

18. Now can you conjugate with the same pronouns in the *pretérito imperfecto?*

19. What does *algo* mean? What type of word is it?

20. What is the relative pronoun *quien* used for? What does it mean?

Now you can go over to the answer key to check how you did!

- If you got 15-20 right answers: Congratulations! You've finished this book, and you have made some great strides in learning Spanish. Keep up the good work, and keep on practicing!

- If you got 10-15 right answers: you're doing great, but maybe you should review the book again (especially any parts you struggled with) to help clear up any doubts or confusion.

- If you got a score below 10: don't get discouraged! You're doing fine, but maybe you need to practice a bit more. I encourage you to go back to the last five chapters and then Chapter 10's revision and take the quiz again!

Vocabulary Appendix

Welcome to the vocabulary appendix! Here, you will find all the vocabulary seen in this book classified by topic. However, you will find the words written in English so you can complete the Spanish part independently.

You can do this once you're done with the book to check your knowledge, or you can complete it as you go!

I recommend you read each chapter while taking notes, then take another day trying to remember everything you've seen in the chapter. Then, on the third day, try to check your knowledge in this section. But it's entirely up to you!

Let's get into the vocabulary and remember that sometimes there is more than one word in Spanish with the same meaning in English!

Colors

- Red:
- Orange
- Yellow:
- Green
- Blue
- Purple
- Pink

- Gray
- Black
- White
- Magenta:
- Light Blue:
- Turquoise:
- Brown

Numbers

- One:
- Two:
- Three
- Four:
- Five:
- Six:
- Seven:
- Eight:
- Nine:
- Ten
- Eleven
- Twelve:
- Thirteen:
- Fourteen:
- Fifteen:
- Sixteen:
- Seventeen:
- Eighteen:
- Nineteen:
- Twenty:
- Twenty-one:
- Twenty-two:
- Twenty-three:

- Twenty-four:
- Twenty-five:
- Twenty-six:
- Twenty-seven:
- Twenty-eight:
- Twenty-nine:
- Thirty:
- Forty:
- Fifty:
- Sixty:
- Eighty:
- Ninety:
- One hundred:

Greetings and Farewells

- Hello:
- Good day:
- Good morning:
- Good evening:
- Good night:
- How are you?:
- Goodbye:
- See you!:
- See you later!:

Introducing ourselves and asking questions

- What's your name?:
- What's your last name?:
- Where are you from?:
- How old are you?:
- What's your nationality?:
- My name is...:
- I'm from...:

- I'm... years old:

Countries and nationalities

- United States:
  - American:
- Spain:
  - Spanish:
- Mexico:
  - Mexican:
- England:
  - English:
- Australia:
  - Australian:
- France:
  - French:
- Colombia:
  - Colombian:
- Peru:
  - Peruvian:
- China:
  - Chinese:
- Brazil:
  - Brazilian:
- Chile:
  - Chilean:
- Argentina:
  - Argentinian:
- Guatemala:
  - Guatemalan:
- Venezuela:
  - Venezuelan:

- Cuba:
  - Cuban:
- South Africa:
  - South African:
- Germany:
  - German:
- Italy:
  - Italian:
- Egypt:
  - Egyptian:
- Greece:
  - Greek:

Booking a Room

- I want to book a room for tonight:
- Do you have any rooms available?:
- I want a single room:
- I'd like a room with a private bathroom:
- What's the price for a double room?:
- Do you have a cheaper option?:
- Can I pay with cash?:
- I only have credit card:
- I would like a room with a view:
- Is breakfast included?:
- At what time is breakfast served?:
- Do you offer airport transfer service?:
- Does the hotel have wifi?:
- Can I see the room?:

Prepositions of Place

- in:
- about:
- to, by, at:

- to the right of:
- near to:
- after:
- in, inside, within:
- on top of:
- toward:

Parts of a House

- front door:
- living room:
- dining-room:
- kitchen:
- storage room:
- fireplace:
- stairs:
- windows:
- hallway:
- garden:
- attic:
- basement:

Objects in the House

- sink:
- faucet:
- stove:
- oven:
- refrigerator:
- freezer:
- dishwasher:
- appliances:
- counter:
- pantry:
- cupboard:

- chair:
- armchair:
- clock:
- coffee table:
- lamp:
- vase:
- carpet:
- bed:
- rug:
- nightlight:
- curtains:
- closet:
- dresser:
- alarm clock:
- towel:
- mirror:
- toothpaste:
- toothbrush:
- soap:
- comb:
- brush:
- razor:
- shaving cream:
- makeup:

Going shopping

- How much is this?:
- How much are those?:
- What's the price?:
- How much?:
- How much is it?:
- The price of that is...:

- It's ...:

Adverbs of Quantity

- many, much, a lot:
- very:
- too much:
- enough, quite:
- somewhat, slightly, a bit:
- little, few:
- more:
- less:
- a lot more:
- so much:
- so many:

Fruits, vegetables, and food

- shellfish:
- octopus:
- stew:
- cake:
- tomato:
- tuna:
- chucken:
- lettuce:
- bread:
- apple:
- rice:
- ham:
- dairy products:
- cheese:
- milk:
- cream:
- yogurt:

- cold cuts:
- fruit:
- vegetable:
- carrot:
- cucumber:
- potato:
- pumpkin:
- pineapple:
- orange:
- strawberry:
- plum:
- egg:
- oil:
- cookie:

Means of Transportation

- train:
- bus:
- airplane:
- taxi:
- bike:
- car:
- motorcycle:
- subway:
- ship:

Buildings

- house:
- apartment:
- museum:
- square:
- cathedral:
- church:

- library:
- cinema:
- supermarket:
- hospital:
- bank:
- restaurant:
- airport:
- train station:
- university:
- pharmacy:

Asking for and giving directions

- Excuse me:
- Where is...?:
- How do I get to...?:
- Could you tell me how to get to...?:
- Is... nearby?:
- Do you know if there is a... nearby?:
- Is... on this street?:
- You have to go straight on:
- Turn left/right:
- Cross the street:
- Continue on this street:
- It's... blocks away:

Adverbs of Place

- here:
- there:
- inside:
- outside:
- ahead:
- behind:
- below:

- above:
- to/on the right:
- to/on the left:
- besides, next to:
- in front of:
- at the end:
- around:
- in the middle:
- near:
- far:
- between:
- on the corner:

Asking for Tickets

- A ticket for..., please:
- Could you give me a ticket for...?:
- Do you have a map of the...?:
- When do you close?:

Time Markers for the Present

- Every day:
- Every Monday:
- Always:
- En general:
- Usualmente:
- Casi nunca:
- Nunca:
- Ahora:
- Ahora mismo:
- En este momento:

Family Members

- grandmother:
- grandfather:

- grandparents:
- mother:
- father:
- parents:
- aunt:
- uncles:
- sister:
- brother:
- female cousin:
- male cousin:
- daughter:
- son:
- granddaughter:
- grandson:
- niece:
- nephew:
- wife:
- husband:
- stepmother:
- stepfather:
- stepsister:
- stepbrother:
- half-sister:
- half-brother:
- stepdaughter:
- stepson:
- godmother:
- godfather:
- goddaughter:
- godson:
- mother-in-law:

- father-in-law:
- sister-in-law:
- brother-in-law:
- daughter-in-law:
- son-in-law:

Adjectives for Describing Appearances

- body shape:
- tall:
- short:
- stout:
- lean:
- lanky:
- slender:
- skinny:
- large:
- petite:
- muscular:
- face:
- bearded:
- square:
- long:
- oval:
- freckled:
- round:
- eyes:
- open:
- blue:
- light-colored:
- brown:
- black:
- dark:

- round:
- green:
- hair:
- thick:
- shiny:
- bald:
- grey:
- brown:
- short:
- frizzy:
- thin:
- straight:
- long:
- black:
- wavy:
- red:
- curly:
- blonde:
- dyed:
- nose:
- hooked:
- wide:
- narrow:
- straight:
- turned-up:
- crooked:
- age:
- old:
- young:
- wrinkly:
- middle-aged:

- youthful:
- elderly:

The Human Body

- body:
- lips:
- back:
- foot:
- finger:
- toe:
- head:
- neck:
- hand:
- leg:
- ankle:
- mouth:
- tooth:
- nail:
- shoulder:
- arm:
- stomach:
- knee:
- lbow:
- ear:

Ordering Food

- A table for two, please:
- What's today's special?:
- What dish do you recommend?:
- What does this dish have?:
- I'm allergic to nuts:
- I'd like a...:
- Could you bring the bill, please?:

Polite Interjections

- sure:
- perfect:
- great:
- right:

Adverbs of Mode

- well:
- bad:
- better:
- worse:
- slowly:
- fast:
- fastly:
- only:
- hardly:
- clearly:
- commonly:
- lately:
- happily:
- timidly:
- simply:

Conjunctions

- or:
- neither, nor:
- because:
- although:
- however:
- as, since, like:
- yet:
- in spite of:
- while:

- when:
- if:

Telling the Time and Date

- in the morning:
- in the afternoon:
- at night:
- it's ... p.m.:
- it's... a.m.:
- What time is it?:
- Do you have the time?:
- Can you tell me what the time is?:
- Monday:
- Tuesday:
- Wednesday:
- Thursday:
- Friday:
- Saturday:
- Sunday:
- January:
- February:
- March:
- April:
- May:
- June:
- July:
- August:
- September:
- October:
- November:
- December:

Ordinal Numbers

- first:
- second:
- third:
- fourth:
- fifth:
- sixth:
- seventh:
- eighth:
- nineth:
- tenth:

Adverbs of Affirmation/Negation/Doubt

- yes:
- of course:
- indeed:
- truly:
- true:
- too:
- not at all:
- never:
- neither:
- nor:
- perhaps, maybe:
- possibly:
- probably:
- surely:

Adjectives for Describing People's Personality

- affectionate:
- good-natured:
- whimsical:
- cowardly:

- gullible:
- cultured:
- miserable:
- absent-minded:
- dignified:
- selfish:
- charming:
- deceitful:
- demanding:
- loyal:
- funny:
- talkative:
- humble:
- clever:
- spoiled:
- prideful:
- smug:
- reserved:
- confident:
- sensible:
- sensitive:
- sincere:
- clumsy:
- hard-working:
- calm:
- courageous:

Seasons

- summer:
- fall:
- winter:
- spring:

Time Expressions for Past Events

- yesterday:
- last night:
- last year:
- last week:
- last month:
- days ago:
- the other day:
- when I was... + age:
- before:
- at that time:
- back then:
- when I was a kid/young:

Jobs/Professions

- student:
- architect:
- engineer:
- lawyer:
- nurse:
- doctor:
- mechanic:
- cook:
- waiter:
- firefighter:
- teacher:
- painter:
- actor/actress:
- singer:
- business person:
- secretary:
- accountant:

- police officer:
- dentist:
- journalist:
- translator:
- vet:

Verbs and Adjectives to Describe a Job

- to sell:
- to call:
- to buy:
- to supervise:
- to drive:
- to write:
- to listen:
- entertaining:
- fun:
- well-paid:
- badly paid:
- stressful:
- difficult:
- demanding:
- enriching:
- repetitive:
- boring:

Answer Key

Spanish Basics

1. jota-u-ele-i-o ese-a-ene-ce-hache-e-zeta.

2. eme-u-jota-e-erre. It doesn't have a *tilde* because it's a *grave* that ends in R.

3. It means that that is the stressed syllable.

4. a. They are all *agudas*.

5. It means that the stressed syllable is the second to last.

6. c. The stressed vowel is the A.

7. It should be a rolled R because all Rs are rolled at the beginning of words.

8. If should be a softer R because a single R in the middle of a word is soft, whereas a double R is a rolled R.

9. /geɾä/ and /goɾilä/. Both are pronounced with a soft G. The U in *guerra* shouldn't be pronounced, and the double R is rolled. The R in *gorila*, however, is softer.

10. It generally comes after.

11. Yes, a pronoun can be the subject of a sentence.

12. False. In Spanish, the subject can be tacit; that is, it can be absent from the sentence because it is already implied in the verb conjugation.

13. No, it doesn't need to change. Unlike English, the order of words can remain the same but we should always include opening and closing question marks.

14. True. Unlike English, in Spanish, the adjectives usually go after the noun.

15. False. The Spanish word for orange is *naranja*. *Amarillo* is the word for yellow.

16. c. Blanco y negro (black and white)

17. Rojo

18. Cuatro

19. Siete

20. Seis (including her)

Meeting New People

1. a. Nos vemos

2. c. Hasta mañana

3. a. ellos is the third person masculine plural pronoun.

4. b. nosotros

5. Masculine nouns usually end in -*O*.

6. To form these plurals, you just need to add an -*S*: *manos, vasos* and *sillas*.

7. c. luces, because the singular form ends in -*Z*.

8. a. verbs don't need to agree in gender with the noun, but they do need to agree in number

9. True. *Estar* is used for temporary states while *ser* is used for permanent ones.

10. False. *Ustedes* is the second person plural pronoun, but it is conjugated in the same way as *ellos* and *ellas*.

11. *Soy* and *estoy*

12. c. *Ella está contenta. Ella* is feminine, so *contenta* should agree in gender and number with her and *contenta* is a temporary state, so we should use *estar* and not *ser*.

13. a. Soy Julio

14. c. Es Sánchez

15. a. Soy de España

---

16. b. Tengo veinte años

17. c. Soy francés

18. Treinta y siete

19. Veintinueve

20. alemana

Checking Into Your Room

1. b. Four

2. The gender and number of the noun define which definite article to use.

3. The Spanish definite articles are *el, los, la* and *las.*

4. False. Spanish has four indefinite articles.

5. The Spanish indefinite articles are *un, unos, una,* and *unas.*

6. c. Una

7. a. Los

8. *Quiero una habitación simple para esta noche, por favor.*

9. True. *Habitación doble* is a room for two people.

10. *Efectivo* and *tarjeta de crédito.*

11. False. To distinguish questions from affirmative sentences, we use the opening and the closing question marks when WRITING Spanish.

12. When speaking, the difference between questions and affirmative sentences is marked through intonation.

13. c. En

14. True. The preposition *a* can mean "to," "by" and "at."

15.

16. Cross the odd one out: d. El jarrón

17. b. Una toalla

18.

19. *Podemos encontrar un espejo* (a mirror) *en el baño, en la sala o en la habitación.*

20. *Podemos encontrar una cama* (a bed) *en la habitación.*

Going Shopping

1. False. To decide which demonstrative pronoun to use, you need to take into account the gender, the number, and the distance from the speaker and the addressee of the noun it's replacing

2. Object close to the speaker, object close to the addressee, object far from both.

3. b. Esa

4. c. Aquellos

5.

6. b. Vale 5€

7. True

8. c. Cuál/cuáles

9. ¿Quiénes vienen a la fiesta?

10. False. *Poco* means "little," "few"

11. c. Nada

12. a. Corremos.

13. Yo canto. Yo bailo

14. Tú bebes. Tú comes

15. Ella sale. Ella vive

16. False. *Zanahoria* meand "carrot"

17. b. Calabaza

18. c. Pastel

19. True

20. c. Aceite

Going Sightseeing

1. *bicicleta*

2. "bus"

3. *museo* and *plaza*

4. "church" and "train station"

5. *Perdone* or *disculpe*

6. ¿*Podría decirme cómo llegar a la biblioteca?* or ¿*Cómo llego a la biblioteca?*

7. *¿Sabe si hay alguna farmacia por aquí?*

8. c. al lado

9. a. en el medio

10. b. cross the street and turn left.

11. *Gira a la derecha y sigue derecho por tres cuadras.*

12. *Tres entradas para el museo, por favor* or *¿Me podría dar tres entradas para el museo?*

13. c. traes

14. b. hemos

15. True.

16. False. if there is a verb that ends in *-ir* or *-er* in the infinitive form, the gerund form ends in *-iendo*. The gerund form ends in *-ando* when there is a verb whose infinitive form ends in *-ar*.

17. *Estoy cantando*

18. a. todos los días

19. c. ahora

20. False. The indicative mode is used for real situations, while the subjunctive mood is used for desires, wishes, suggestions or hypotheses.

Quiz

1. Gorrión is an *aguda*. It should be pronounced with a soft G and a strong/rolled R.

2. The sentence is grammatically incorrect because the verbs should agree in number with Lucía (third-person singular) and the adjective should agree in gender and number with Lucía (feminine third-person singular). A grammatically correct sentence would be: *Lucía juega al fútbol, es muy buena.*

3. You can ask using the phrase *¿Cuántos años tienes?* and answer with *Tengo...* and the number of years

4. The Spanish indefinite articles are *un, unos, una* and *unas*. We use *un* with masculine singular nouns, *unos* with masculine plural nouns, *una* with feminine singular nouns, and *unas* with feminine plural nouns.

5. *¿Puedo pagar en efectivo?*

6. You use the same sentence as in the affirmative but add opening and closing question marks.

7. We would use the preposition *hacia*: *Camino hacia el museo.*

8. c. cama. The bed does not belong in the bathroom.

9. You should take into account the gender, number and the distance from the speaker.

10. We could ask *¿Cuánto cuesta/vale/sale el pollo?*, *¿Qué precio tiene el pollo?*, *¿Cuál es el precio del pollo?* or even *¿A qué precio está el pollo?* The store clerk could answer *Vale/cuesta/sale 20€, son 20€* or *El precio del pollo es 20€.*

11. *Cuánto* means "how much." However, *cuántos* means "how many." It is not the plural equivalent of *cuánto*.

12. *¿Por qué están tan caras las calabazas?*

13. *¿Dónde están los pasteles?*

14. We would use the adverbs *demasiado* and *poco*: *Es demasiado para unos pocos días.*

15. *Yo amo, tú amas, ella ama, nosotras amamos, vosotras amáis,* and *ellas aman.*

16. *Yo temo, tú temes, él teme, nosotros tememos, vosotros teméis,* and *ellos temen.*

17. *Yo parto, tú partes, ella parte, nosotras partimos, vosotras partís,* and *ellas parten.*

18. We could ask *¿Cómo llego al supermercado?* or *¿Podría decirme cómo llegar al supermercado?* And we could answer *Tienes que doblar/girar a la derecha, seguir derecho por tres cuadras y luego doblar/girar a la izquierda.*

19. he conjugation of the verb *ser* is: *Yo soy, tú eres, él es, nosotros somos, vosotros sois,* and *ellos son.* And the conjugation of the verb *estar* is: *yo estoy, tú estás, él está, nosotros estamos, vosotros estáis,* and *ellos están.*

20. The first one is in the present form and the second one is in the present progressive form. The present progressive is formed by the conjugation of the verb *estar* and a gerund.

Having a House Party

1. False. *Abuela* means grandmother, and *abuelo* means grandfather.
2. d. Tío
3. True. *Marido* and *esposo* both mean "husband."
4. The Spanish word to talk about your children's female partner is *nuera*.
5. The Spanish word to talk about your partner's father is *suegro*.
6. False. *Esbelto/a* and *bajo/a* are used to describe the body shapes. *Rizado/a* is used to describe hair.
7. True. *Canoso/a, arrugado/a* and *entrado/a en años* are things you would say to describe an elder person.
8. All of the adjectives mentioned can be used to describe a feminine noun.
9. The Spanish word for "mouth" is *boca*.
10. c. Cabello
11. False. Possessive pronouns replace the noun and are used together with a definite article.
12. Possessive pronouns and adjectives agree with the noun they refer to.
13. The possessive adjectives equivalent to English "my" are *mi* and *mis*.
14. The definite article that comes before the possessive pronoun *suyos* is *los*.
15. b. La
16. True. The direct object is the person or thing that receives the action of the verb.
17. The direct object pronoun needs to agree in gender and number with the noun it's replacing.
18. *Lo compró hace poco.*
19. True. The indirect object is the person or thing the action is intended to benefit or harm.
20. d. Las

Eating Out

1. False. *Desayuno* is in the morning and *Merienda* is in the afternoon

2. *Mi comida preferida es el espagueti* or *Mi comida favorita es el espagueti*

3. False. *Encantar* means "to love" and *gustar* means "to like"

4. a. encanta

5. b. Me gustan las ostras

6. c. A ellos les gusta la paella

7. b. No le gusta comer pasta

8. a. Esta camisa es más pequeña que aquella

9. a. Me gusta menos la mesa que la silla

10. c. Érica es mayor que Carlos

11. c. Este libro es peor que el anterior

12. False. *Primeros* is the starter and *segundos* is the main course

13. b. ¿Qué trae este plato?

14. *Yo quiero una pizza*

15. *¿Podría traer la cuenta, por favor?*

16. *Bien*

17. a. the feminine form of the adjective + *-mente*

18. It means "or"

19. d. *porque*

20. It means "if" and it is different from *sí*, which means "yes"

Booking Tickets

1. True

2. c. *de la mañana*

3. b. *de la tarde*

4. a. *de la noche*

5. *Son las ocho de la mañana*

6. b. *Es la una de la mañana*

7. *Mediodía*

8. *Lunes, martes, miércoles, jueves, viernes, sábado, domingo.*

9. *Enero, febrero, marzo, abril, mayo, junio, julio, agosto, septiembre, octubre, noviembre, diciembre.*

10.

11. b. *Quinto*

12. False.

13. True.

14. d. All of the previous

15. *Gustaré, gustarás, gustará, gustaremos, gustaréis, gustarán.*

16. *Leeré, leerás, leerá, leeremos, leeréis, leerán.*

17. c. *En efecto*

18. False.

19. Egoísta

20.

Talking About Your Past

1. *Invierno* comes before *primavera*, and *verano* comes before *otoño.*

2. b. to talk about past events

3. False. That is the case for the *pretérito imperfecto*

4. True.

5. a. to talk about past habits

6. True.

7. a. amabas

8. The *pretérito perfecto simple* because it is an isolated event.

9. The *pretérito imperfecto* because it is something that used to happen often in the past.

10. b. estuvimos

11. The *pretérito perfecto simple*

12. The *pretérito imperfecto*

13. c. hace días

14. d. nothing

15. c. none

16. Yes, it does

17. *cuyo, cuya, cuyos,* or *cuyas*

18. a. Los lugares que visité en España son hermosos

19. d. empresario/a

20. c. en

Quiz

1. *Julia es mi tía*

2. You can use the phrase *"mi cara es"* with the adjectives: *barbuda, cuadrada, redonda, larga, ovala, pecosa* or *redonda.*

3. *cabeza, hombros, rodillas y dedos del pie*

4. *el mío, la mía, los míos, las mías*

5. *nos*

6. *les*

7. *Me gustan las lentejas, pero no me encanta el gazpacho*

8. *Esta es la mejor paella del mundo*

9. *Una mesa para cuatro, por favor*

10. *difícilmente*

11. *Hoy es domingo 18 de julio de 2021*

12. *cantaré, cantarás, cantará, cantaremos, cantaréis, cantarán*

13. *Mañana vamos a cantar toda la noche*

14. *En absoluto* is an adverb of negation and means "not at all"

15. "clumsy"

16. The *pretérito perfecto simple* is used to talk about single events in the past, while the *pretérito imperfecto* is used to talk about past habits.

17. *salí, saliste, salió, salimos, salisteis, salieron*

18. *salía, salías, salía, salíamos, salíais, salían*

19. *algo* means "something" and it is an indefinite pronoun.

20. It is used to talk about a person and it means "who."

Extra: IPA Phonemic Chart

Hi! It's Julio here again. I've come to teach you the Spanish phonemes. The IPA (International Phonetic Alphabet) is made up of symbols used to describe language sounds. The sounds used in Spanish are very different from those used in English. The symbols may appear a bit difficult to understand, but I've got you covered! I'll make it clear and simple for you to understand so you can go back to this page anytime you need to.

This is a simplified Spanish IPA chart:

Vowels	ä (sala)	e̯ (querer)	i (iris)	o̯ (oso)	u (luz)
Consonants	b (futbol)	β (bebé)	d (cuando)	ð (dado)	f (foco)
	g (gota)	j (ayuda)	k (caja)	l (leer)	ʎ (llave)
	m (mala)	n (nene)	ɲ (ñandú)	ŋ (tengo)	p (papel)
	r (barro)	ɾ (caro)	s (seco)	θ (zorro)	t (torta)
	tʃ (charco)	v (afgano)	x (mojar)	ʃ (show)	

I know, it looks like a lot! But do not fret! Let's break it down so you can understand it and make the most of it.

Let's start with the vowels. To be honest, none of the Spanish vowels sounds exactly like any English vowel. But here's a trick to attempting a better pronunciation that worked for Sarah:

- /a/: It sounds like the A in "father," only Spanish A is a bit shorter.

- /e/: It sounds like the E in "men," only your tongue should be a bit forward.

- /i/: It sounds like the EE in "see," only shorter.

- /o/: It sounds like the O in "pot," only the sound isn't made from the very back of the throat but from the middle of the mouth.

- /u/: It sounds like the OO in "soothe," only shorter.

Consonants are a bit more complicated because, depending on the region, their pronunciation may vary greatly. But let's try to make the chart above a bit simpler:

- /b/: This phoneme is the same as the English B in "but" and is generally used when there's a V or a B at the beginning of a word or after a consonant. Did you notice that I said a V or a B? Well, that's because there isn't a phonetic difference between the two in Spanish. They sound the same! Consider that in Spanish, we shouldn't blow that much air when pronouncing this consonant.

- /β/: This phoneme is also used for Bs and is used in many instances in Spanish, but it doesn't sound like the English B. It is between an English B and a V, but your lips shouldn't touch, and your teeth shouldn't touch your lower lip either.

- /d/: This sound does have an English counterpart; it is the D sound in "dog." However, many Spanish learners tend to use it everywhere they see a D when, most often than not, they should use the /ð/ sound. The /d/ sound is generally used only after some consonants.

- /ð/: This sound also exists in English; it is the TH sound in "this." When we see a D, we should probably pronounce it like a TH. To remember how to pronounce this consonant, remember that *madre* and "mother" use the same sound!

- /f/: This sound is pronounced the same as the English F in "follow," and you can use it almost every time you see an F in Spanish. There's finally one that gives us a break, right?

- /g/: For this consonant, there is also an English equivalent; it sounds just like the G in "goat." However, like in English, not all Gs sound the same in Spanish. When G is followed by E or I, it is pronounced with this phoneme: /x/

- /ʝ/: This is a sound that isn't used by all Spanish speakers, and it doesn't have an English equivalent, but it is between the "j" sound in "jeep" and the "y" sound in "yet." Those who use this sound use it whenever a vowel follows a Y.

- /k/: This sound is the same as the English C in "cat." It is used when the letter C is followed by A, O, or U and whenever there's a letter K.

- /l/: This is the same sound as the English L in "light." The letter L always has this sound, except when it is doubled.

- /ʎ/: This sound is very similar to the sound of the Y in "yet," only it is a bit more open. It is used in some places whenever there is a double L. However, in some other places, the double L may be pronounced with a /ʝ/ sound or a /ʃ/ sound.

- /m/: This is another straightforward sound, thankfully. This is the same as the M sound in "mole" and is used whenever there is an M in Spanish.

- /n/: The N sound in "nice" is the same as this! And it is used whenever there is an N in Spanish.

- /ɲ/: This may be a tricky sound because neither the letter Ñ nor the /ɲ/ sound exist in English. This phoneme sounds a bit like an N followed by a Y, like in the last name of actress Lupita Nyong'o, or the name of the artist Kanye West. It is used whenever there is an Ñ.

- /ŋ/: Like in Spanish, this sound is used whenever there is an N and a G together, like in any "-ing" ending, or an N and a K together.

- /p/: This sound is also the same in English as it is in Spanish, but, like the /b/, in Spanish, we shouldn't blow as much air when we pronounce it. It is used whenever there is a P, and it sounds like the P in "point."

- /r/: For English speakers, this is a tough one. This sound is used whenever a word starts with R, or when there is a double R. To pronounce it, your tongue should be in the same position as when you pronounce the English R, but you have to make a trill between your tongue and ridge of bone behind your teeth. It may take practice to master it, but I know you can learn to roll your Rs.

- /ɾ/: In English, this is called a voiced alveolar tap, and it is the TT sound used by some English speakers, like Americans, when they say "better." In Spanish, it is used whenever there is a single R in the middle of a word.

- /s/: Another sound that is the same in English as in Spanish! This one is the S sound in "see" and, in Spanish, is used whenever there is an S at the beginning of a word (unless it is followed by an H).

- /θ/: This is the sound that Spanish people use when a word starts with a C followed by I or E, or when there is an S or a Z after a vowel. And it sounds like the TH sound in "thing."

- /t/: This is the T sound used in "stay." And in Spanish, it is used for all Ts.

- /tʃ/: Whenever there is a CH in Spanish, this phoneme is used, and it sounds like the CH in "choose."

- /v/: This is not a common sound in Spanish; it is used only when a G follows the F.

- /x/: This sound does not exist in English, but it is similar to the H sound in "hall," only it is a bit stronger. It is used when an E or an I follow a J or a G. Sometimes, although it is an exception, it can be the sound of the X in words like "México."

- /ʃ/: This is the sound of the SH in "show," and, in Spanish, it is used whenever there is an SH. As we've mentioned, it is also used in some places when there is an LL.

I hope this has made Spanish pronunciation a bit easier for you. Remember that practice makes perfect, so once you get acquainted with the phonemes and with the language, you'll definitely be a pro!

Extra: Glossary of Grammatical Terms

Before saying goodbye, I wanted to share the glossary of grammatical terms I have been compiling with the words Julio used during the trip. I hope you find it helpful!

adjective (adjetivo): a word that modifies a noun or its referent.

adverb (adverbio): a word that modifies a verb, an adjective or another adverb.

affirmative sentence (oración afirmativa): a sentence that states something; it expresses validity of truth.

agreement (concordancia): the correspondence in some grammatical feature (number, gender or person) between words.

article (artículo): the words used together with nouns to limit them, such as "a," "an," and "the."

cardinal number (número cardinal): a number used in simple counting, and to indicate how many elements there are in a group.

clause (cláusula): a group of words that have a subject and a predicate, and are part of a larger sentence.

common noun (sustantivo común): a noun that refers to a class of entities and is used to designate instances of a class of beings or things.

comparative (comparativo): related to or constituting the intermediate degree of comparison of adjectives.

complement of the verb (complemento del verbo): a word, phrase, or clause that is necessary to complete the meaning of the verb.

conjugation (conjgación): the way in which we change the form of a verb to reflect tense, aspect, mood, voice, and person.

conjunction (conjunción): the words we use to join two or more elements, clauses, or sentences, such as "and," "but," "because," and "however."

definite article (artículo definido): an article put before a noun when the identity of the noun is known to the addressee.

demonstrative article (artículo demostrativo): a word that modifies a noun while it points out the one referred to, and distinguishes it from others.

demonstrative pronoun (pronombre demostrativo): the words we use to point out the one referred to, and to distinguish it from others.

diaeresis (diéresis): an orthographic mark (¨) used on top of vowels to indicate a change in pronunciation.

dialect (dialecto): a regional variety of language.

direct object (objeto directo): the noun or noun group which is directly affected by or involved in the action of the verb.

gender (género): a grammatical subclass, partly arbitrary and partly based on distinguishable characteristics, such as biological sex, which determines agreement with and selection of other words (such as nouns, pronouns, articles, adjectives, etc.)

gerund (gerundio): a nonpersonal form of the verb, which in English ends in -ing and, in Spanish, in -ndo, used in verbal periphrasis or as a modifier with adverbial nature.

graphic accent (tilde): Spanish orthographic mark (´) used to show the accented syllable or as a diacritic.

imperative (imperativo): the grammatical mood that expresses the will to influence the behavior of the addressee.

indefinite article (artículo indefinido): an article used before a noun when the identity of the noun is unknown to the addressee.

indefinite pronoun (pronombre indefinido): a word that doesn't have a specific familiar referent, and that's used to talk about people or things, or to express some quantity in a vague or general way.

indicative (indicativo): the grammatical mood which expresses that what's said by the predicate is believed to be factual information.

indirect object (objeto indirecto): is the person or thing that the action of the verb is intended to benefit or harm.

infinitive (infinitivo): a nonpersonal form of the verb, which in Spanish, ends in -ar, -er, or -ir, used in verbal periphrasis or as a modifier with noun nature.

interrogative pronoun (pronombre interrogativo): a pronoun used to ask questions; they are used for reference to people or to things.

intonation (entonación): the fall and rise in pitch of the voice when talking.

irregular verb (verbo irregular): a verb that doesn't conform to the usual pattern of inflection.

mood (modo): a grammatical feature of verbs that signals modality, that is, the attitude of the speaker toward what they are saying (for example, is it a fact, a desire, a command?)

noun (sustantivo): a type of word that works as the name of an object or set of objects, such as: living creatures, actions, qualities, places, or concepts.

number (número): a grammatical category of different types of words (nouns, pronouns, adjectives, and verbs) that expresses count distinctions; in English and Spanish, number can be singular or plural.

object pronoun (pronombre de objeto): a personal pronoun normally used as the direct or indirect object of a verb, or as the object of a preposition.

ordinal number (número ordinal): a number used to represent the position or rank of a noun.

person (persona): the grammatical distinction between those speaking (first person), those being addressed (second person), and those who are neither speaking nor being addressed (third person).

phoneme (fonema): in a given language, a unit of sound that can distinguish two words.

possessive adjective (adjetivo posesivo): a type of adjective that modifies a noun by identifying who has ownership or possession over it.

possessive pronoun (pronombre posesivo): a type of pronoun that shows a noun's ownership or possession.

predicate (predicado): a part of a sentence or clause that contains a verb, and states something about the subject.

pronoun (pronombre): a word used as a substitute for a noun or a noun phrase; it's used to refer to people, animals or things without naming them, when the referent has been named or is understood from context.

proper noun (nombre propio): a word or group of words that designate a particular person, place, or thing, and is usually capitalized in English.

regular verb (verbo regular): a verb that follows the usual pattern of inflection when it's conjugated, without modifying its root.

relative clause (oración de relativo): a type of clause that compliments a noun or a noun phrase.

relative pronoun (pronombre relativo): a grammatical device used to introduce a relative clause.

root (raíz): the element from which a word is derived by phonetic change or by extension.

sentence (oración): a grammatical structure formed by the union of a subject and a predicate; in writing, it usually begins with a capital letter and concludes with end punctuation.

stressed syllable (sílaba tónica): the syllable of a word that carries the phonetic emphasis or prominence.

subject (sujeto): a noun, pronoun, or noun phrase that designates the entity of which something is predicated.

subject pronoun (pronombres de sujeto): a personal pronoun normally used as the subject of a clause.

superlative (superlativo): related to or constituting the degree of comparison that denotes an extreme or unsurpassed level or extent of adjectives.

tense (tiempo): a category of the verb that expresses a distinction of time or duration of the action or state denoted by that verb.

time marker (marcador temporal): a word or expression used in discourse to indicate time.

verb (verbo): a word that is the center of a predicate and that's inflected for agreement, tense, voice, mood, or aspect.

www.ingramcontent.com/pod-product-compliance
Lightning Source LLC
LaVergne TN
LVHW051735080426
835511LV00018B/3065